THE
EASY WAY TO
STOP
SMOKING

THE
EASY WAY TO
STOP
SMOKING

ALLEN CARR

STERLING

New York / London
www.sterlingpublishing.com

DEDICATION

To the smokers I have failed to cure,
I hope it will help them to get free.

And to Sid Sutton

But most of all to Joyce

Library of Congress Cataloging-in-Publication Data Available

4   6   8   10   9   7   5   3

Published by Sterling Publishing Co., Inc.
387 Park Avenue South, New York, NY 10016

©1985, 1991, 1998, 2004 by Allen Carr's Easyway (International) Ltd.

Allen Carr's Easyway and **Easyway**™ are trademarks of
Allen Carr's Easyway (International) Ltd.

Sterling ISBN 978-1-4027-1861-8 (hardcover)

Sterling ISBN 978-1-4027-7163-7 (paperback)

For information about custom editions, special sales, premium and
corporate purchase, please contact Sterling Special Sales Department at
800-805-5480 or specialsales@sterlingpublishing.com

The information contained in this book is not intended to replace the services
of trained health professionals or be a substitute for medical advice.

About the Author

Allen Carr was a highly successful businessman, but his hundred-cigarettes-a-day habit was driving him to despair when, after a third of a century of nicotine addiction and countless failed attempts at quitting, he discovered what the world had been waiting for—the Easy Way to Stop Smoking.

Although devised to treat his own dependence, the effectiveness of his approach convinced him that his method could be used to help others as well, and he left his job to begin a personal crusade to cure the world's smokers. Encouraged by the outstanding success of Easy Way, Allen started building the network of clinics bearing his name that now spans the globe. Allen has since established an unparalleled reputation, and Easy Way is now recognized around the world as the foremost method for stopping smoking.

The phenomenal success of the method is based on word of mouth and recommendation; to this day Easy Way does not advertise. The *Easy Way to Stop Smoking* is now an international best seller, having sold over five million copies in more than twenty languages. The global network of Easy Way clinics also continues to grow, most recently in the United States. Information about the Easy Way method and the expansion of the clinic network in the USA can be found online at www.allencarrusa.com.

CONTENTS

Foreword to the 20th Anniversary Edition

This edition of EASYWAY celebrates the twentieth anniversary of the discovery of my method, which shows you just how easy and enjoyable it is to stop smoking. As I sit at my state-of-the-art laptop, it is difficult to believe that the original manuscript of this work was handwritten, barely legible—least of all to the writer—and then typed up on an ancient Underwood. When I extinguished my final cigarette on July 15, 1983, I knew for certain that I had discovered something that every smoker was searching for: an easy and immediate method to escape from nicotine slavery. What I didn't know for certain was whether I could convince a single smoker, let alone the world.

EASYWAY has exceeded all of my expectations. I am now widely recognized as the world's leading expert on stopping smoking. My book has sold around five million copies and has been translated into more than twenty languages. In the UK, it has been a bestseller every year since its publication in 1987. It has also been a bestseller in Germany, the Netherlands, Norway, Japan, France, Spain, and the Republic of Ireland. However, the real satisfaction I get from my work is the knowledge that every day it helps thousands of smokers escape from the slavery of smoking.

It all started with just my wife Joyce and myself at our home in London. Today we have a network of more than fifty EASYWAY Clinics in twenty countries worldwide. My thirty years of chain-smoking were a nightmare, and I am pleased to have this opportunity to thank my colleagues, my publishers, and the millions of ex-smokers who have quit with the help of EASYWAY. They, combined with my freedom from the weed, have made the last twenty years seem like paradise.

I hope that this edition of my little book will help to rescue millions of Americans from an addiction that has already claimed more lives than all the wars of history put together.

—Allen Carr, May 2004

Preface

At last the miracle cure all smokers have been waiting for:

- Instantaneous
- Equally effective for the light or heavy smoker
- No bad withdrawal pangs
- No willpower required
- No shock treatment
- No aids or gimmicks required
- No weight gain
- Permanent

Perhaps you are somewhat apprehensive about reading this book. Perhaps, like the majority of smokers, the mere thought of stopping fills you with panic, and although you have every intention of stopping one day, today is not that day.

If you are expecting me to inform you of the terrible health risks that smokers run, that smokers spend a small fortune during their smoking lives, that it is a filthy, disgusting habit, and that you are a stupid, spineless, weak-willed jellyfish, then I must disappoint you. Those tactics never helped me to quit, and if they were going to help you, you would already have quit.

My method, which I call EASYWAY, doesn't work that way. You might find some of the things that I am about to say difficult to believe. However, by the time you've finished this book, you'll not only believe them, but you'll also wonder how you could ever have been brainwashed into believing otherwise.

There is a common misapprehension that we choose to smoke. Smokers no more choose to smoke than alcoholics choose to become alcoholics, or heroin addicts choose to become heroin addicts. It is true that we choose to light those first experimental cigarettes. I occasionally choose to go to the movies, but I certainly didn't choose to spend my whole life in a movie theater.

Please reflect on your life. Did you ever make the positive decision that at certain times in your life you couldn't enjoy a meal or a social occasion without smoking, or that you couldn't concentrate or handle stress without a cigarette? At what stage did you decide that you needed cigarettes, not just for social occasions, but permanently in your presence, and felt insecure, even panic-stricken, without them?

Like every other smoker, you have been lured into the most sinister, subtle trap that man and nature have combined to devise. There is not a parent on this planet, whether smoker or non-smoker, who likes the thought of his or her children smoking. This means that all smokers wish they had never started. Not surprising, really—no one needs cigarettes to enjoy meals or cope with stress before he or she gets hooked.

At the same time, all smokers wish to continue to smoke. After all, no one forces us to keep lighting up; whether we understand the reason or not, it is only smokers themselves who decide to light up.

If there were a magic button that smokers could press to wake up the following morning as if they had never lit that first cigarette, the only smokers who would remain tomorrow morning would be those who are still at the experimental stage. The only thing that prevents us from quitting is: FEAR!

Fear that we will have to survive an indeterminate period of misery, deprivation, and unsatisfied craving in order to be free. Fear that a meal or social occasion will never be quite as enjoyable without a cigarette. Fear that we'll never be able to concentrate, handle stress, or be as confident without our little crutch. Fear that our personality and character will change. But most of all, the fear of "once a smoker, always a smoker"—that we will never be completely free and will spend the rest of our lives craving the occasional cigarette.

If, as I did, you have already tried all the conventional ways to quit and have been through the misery of what I describe as the willpower method of stopping, you will not only be affected by that fear, but you'll also be convinced you can never quit.

If you are apprehensive, panic-stricken, or feel that the time is not right for you to give up, then let me assure you that your apprehension or panic is caused by fear. That fear is not relieved by cigarettes, but created by them. You didn't decide to fall into the nicotine trap. But like all traps, it is designed to ensure that you remain trapped. Ask yourself, when you lit those first experimental cigarettes, did you decide to remain a smoker as long as you have? So when are you going to quit? Tomorrow? Next year? Stop kidding yourself! The trap is designed to hold you for life. Why else do you think all these other smokers don't quit before it kills them?

This book was first published in 1985 and has appeared constantly on the bestseller lists since then. I now have almost twenty years' feedback, and as you will soon see, the feedback has revealed information that has exceeded my wildest aspirations of the effectiveness of my method. It has also revealed two aspects of EASYWAY that have caused me concern. The second I will be covering later. The first arose from the letters that I have received. Here are three typical examples:

"I didn't believe the claims you made and I apologize for doubting you. It was just as easy and enjoyable as you said it would be. I've given copies of your book to all my smoking friends and relatives, but I can't understand why they don't read it."

"I was given your book eight years ago by an ex-smoking friend. I've just got around to reading it. My only regret is that I wasted eight years."

"I've just finished reading EASYWAY. I know it has only been four days, but I feel so great, I know I'll never need to smoke again. I first

started to read your book five years ago, got halfway through and panicked. I knew that if I went on reading I would have to stop. Wasn't I silly?"

No, that particular young woman wasn't silly. I've referred to a magic button. EASYWAY works just like that magic button. Let me make it quite clear: EASYWAY isn't magic, but for me and the hundreds of thousands of ex-smokers who have found it so easy and enjoyable to quit, it seems like magic!

Every smoker wants to quit and every smoker can find it easy and enjoyable to quit. It's only fear that prevents them from doing so. We have a chicken and egg situation. The greatest gain is to be rid of that fear. But you won't be free of that fear until you complete the book. On the contrary, like the woman in the third example, your fear might increase as you read the book and it might prevent you from finishing it.

You didn't decide to fall into the trap, but be clear in your mind, you won't escape from it unless you make a positive decision to do so. You might already be straining at the leash to quit. On the other hand you might be apprehensive. Either way please bear in mind: YOU HAVE ABSOLUTELY NOTHING TO LOSE!

If, at the end of this book, you decide that you wish to continue to smoke, there is nothing to prevent you from doing so. You don't even have to cut down or stop smoking while you are reading this book, and remember, there is no shock treatment. On the contrary, I have only good news for you. Can you imagine how the Count of Monte Cristo felt when he finally escaped from that prison? That's how I felt when I escaped from the nicotine trap. That's how the millions of ex-smokers who have used my method feel. By the end of this book: THAT'S HOW YOU WILL FEEL!

GO FOR IT!

If you are a smoker all you have to do is read on.

If you are a non-smoker buying this book for loved ones, all you have to do is persuade them to read it. If you cannot persuade them, then read the book yourself, and the last chapter will advise you how to get the message across—and how to prevent your children from starting. Do not be fooled by the fact that your kids say they hate smoking now. All children do before they become hooked.

Introduction

"I'M GOING TO CURE THE WORLD OF SMOKING."
One day I told my wife that I'd just smoked my last cigarette, and she thought that I had flipped. Her reaction was understandable if you consider that she had watched me fail numerous attempts to quit. The most recent attempt had been two years previously. I'd actually survived six months of sheer purgatory before I finally succumbed and lit a cigarette. I'm not ashamed to admit that I cried like a baby. I was crying because I knew that I was condemned to be a smoker for life. I'd put so much effort into that attempt and suffered so much misery that I knew I would never have the strength to go through that ordeal again. I'm not a violent man, but if some patronizing non-smoker had been stupid enough at that moment to suggest to me that all smokers can find it easy to quit, immediately and perma-nently, I would not have been responsible for my actions. However, I'm convinced that any jury in the world, comprised of smokers only, would have pardoned me on the grounds of justifiable homicide.

Perhaps you, too, find it impossible to believe that any smoker can find it easy to quit. If so, I beg you not to cast this book into the trash bin. Please trust me. I assure you that even you can find it easy to quit.

Anyway, there I was two years later, having just extinguished what I knew would be my final cigarette, not only telling my wife that I was already a non-smoker, but that I was going to cure the rest of the world. I must admit that at the time I found her skepti-cism somewhat irritating. However, in no way did it diminish my feeling of exaltation. I suppose that my exhilaration in knowing that I was already a happy non-smoker distorted my perspective somewhat. With the benefit of hindsight, I can sympathize with her attitude, I now understand why my wife and my close friends and relatives thought I was a candidate for the funny farm.

As I look back on my life, it seems that my whole existence has been a preparation for solving the smoking problem. Even those hateful years of training and practicing as an accountant were invaluable in helping me unravel the mysteries of the smoking trap. They say you can't fool all the people all of the time, but I believe the tobacco companies have done just that for years. I also believe that I am the first to really understand the smoking trap. If I appear to be arrogant, let me hasten to add that it was no credit to me, just the circumstances of my life.

The momentous day was July 15, 1983. It wasn't quite like Nelson Mandela finally leaving prison, but I imagine he felt the same sense of relief and exhilaration as I did when I extinguished that final cigarette. I realized I had discovered something that every smoker was praying for: an easy way to stop smoking.

After testing out the method on smoking friends and relatives, I gave up accounting and became a full-time consultant, helping other smokers become free.

My inspiration for the first edition of this book is a man I describe in chapter 25. He visited me twice, and we were both reduced to tears on each occasion. He was so agitated that he couldn't relax enough to absorb what I was saying. I hoped that if I wrote it all down, he could read it in his own good time, as many times as he wanted to, and absorb the message.

I had no doubt that EASYWAY would work just as effectively for other smokers as it had for me. However, when I contemplated putting the method into book form, I was apprehensive. I did my own market research. The comments were not very encouraging:

"How can a book help me quit? What I need is willpower!"
"How can a book avoid the terrible withdrawal pangs?"

In addition to these pessimistic comments, I had my own doubts. Often at the clinics it became obvious that a client had misunderstood an important point that I was making. I was able to correct the situation. But how would a book be able to do that? I remembered well the frustrating times when I studied to qualify as an accountant, when I didn't understand or agree with a particular point in a book and couldn't ask the book to explain. I was also well aware, particularly in these days of television and videos, that many people are not accustomed to reading.

And I had one doubt that overrode all these other factors. I wasn't a writer and was very conscious of my limitations in this respect. I was confident that I could sit down face to face with a smoker and convince that smoker how much more enjoyable social occasions would be, how he or she would be better able to concentrate and handle stress as a non-smoker, and just how easy and enjoyable the process of quitting could be. But could I transfer that facility to a book? I even doubted whether I had the right to put EASYWAY into book form and wondered whether I should have employed a professional writer. In no way was I certain that it would be a success.

Thankfully the gods were kind to me. I've received thousands of complimentary letters containing comments such as:

> *"It's the greatest book ever written."*
> *"You are my guru."*
> *"You are a genius."*
> *"You should be knighted."*
> *"You should be prime minister."*
> *"You are a saint."*

I hope that I have not allowed such comments to go to my head. I'm fully aware that those comments were made not to compliment me on my literary skills, but in spite of my lack of them. They were made because whether your preference is to read a book or to attend a clinic: the EASYWAY system works!

Not only do we now have a worldwide network of EASYWAY clinics, but this book has also been translated into more than twenty languages, and it features constantly on the nonfiction bestseller lists across Europe.

After approximately a year of running smoking clinics, I thought I had learned everything that was possible to learn about helping smokers quit. Amazingly, almost twenty years after discovering the method, I still learn something new practically every day. This fact caused me some concern when I was asked to revise the first edition after six years of publication. I feared that practically everything I had written would have to be amended or retracted.

I needn't have worried. The basic principles of EASYWAY are as sound today as when I first discovered the method. The beautiful truth is: IT IS EASY TO STOP!

That is a fact. My only difficulty is to convince every smoker of that fact. All of the knowledge that I have accumulated over the course of twenty years has helped enable every smoker to see the light. At our clinics we try to achieve perfection. Every failure hurts us deeply because we know every smoker can find it easy to quit. When smokers fail, they tend to regard it as their failure. We regard it as our failure—we failed to convince those smokers just how easy and enjoyable it is to quit.

I dedicated the first edition to the smokers that I had failed to cure. That failure rate was based on the money-back guarantee that we give at our clinics. The average current failure rate of our clinics worldwide is under ten percent. That means a success rate of over ninety percent.

Today we have a network of more than fifty EASYWAY clinics in twenty countries worldwide—in cities as diverse as New York City, Milan, London, Chicago, Toronto, Capetown, Paris, and Madrid, my clinics have successfully operated for twenty years.

Smokers arrive at my clinics in differing states of panic, convinced they won't succeed in stopping, and believing that even if they do stop they will have to endure a terrible period of abject misery, that social occasions will never be quite so enjoyable, that they will be less able to concentrate and cope with stress, and that, although they might never smoke again, they will never be completely free, and for the rest of their lives, they will have occasional yearnings for cigarettes and will have to resist the temptation.

The majority of those smokers leave the clinics a few hours later already happy non-smokers. How do we achieve that miracle? You need to book an appointment at your nearest EASYWAY clinic to find out. The clinics enjoy such a high success rate that we are able to give a money-back guarantee. The fee varies according to location, and if you belong to the twenty percent who require more than one visit, you can attend any number of follow-ups without further charge. We never give up on any smoker. And if you decide, having attended three sessions within three months without cancellation, that you no longer wish to stop, your fee will be refunded in full. On the basis of our money-back guarantee, the worldwide success rate at our clinics averages over ninety percent.

Don't be mistaken—the success of the clinics should not detract from the value of this book, which in itself has enabled millions of smokers to stop. If you are in doubt, why not telephone your nearest EASYWAY clinic for further guidance. A list of clinics appears at the back of the book.

Although I was aware that I had discovered something marvelous, I never in my wildest dreams expected to achieve such rates. You might well argue that if I genuinely believed that I would cure the world of smoking, I must have expected to achieve one hundred percent.

No, I never ever expected to achieve one hundred percent. Snuff-taking was the previous most popular form of nicotine addiction until it became antisocial. However, there are still a few weirdos who continue to take snuff, and probably there always will be. Amazingly, Britain's Houses of Parliament are one of the last bastions of snuff-taking. I suppose this is not so surprising when you think about it; politicians are generally about a hundred years behind the times. So there will always be a few weirdos that will continue to smoke. I certainly never expected to cure every smoker personally.

I naively thought that the rest of the world would also see the light and adopt my method once I had explained the mysteries of the smoking trap and dispelled such illusions as:

- Smokers enjoy smoking.
- Smokers choose to smoke.
- Smoking relieves boredom and stress.
- Smoking aids concentration and relaxation.
- Smoking is a habit.
- It takes willpower to quit.
- Once a smoker always a smoker.
- Telling smokers that it kills them helps them to quit.
- Substitutes, particularly nicotine replacement, help smokers quit.
- Smokers have to go through a transitional period of misery in order to quit.

I thought my chief antagonist would be the tobacco industry. Amazingly, my chief stumbling blocks were the very institutions I assumed would be my greatest allies: the media, the government, organizations like the American Cancer Society, and the established medical profession.

The movie *Sister Kenny* (1946), about infantile paralysis, or polio, illustrates exactly the attitude I encountered. I vividly remember that the word "polio" engendered the same fear in me then as the word "cancer" does now. Polio not only paralyzed the legs and arms, but also distorted the limbs. The established medical treatment was to put affected limbs in irons and thus prevent the distortion. The result was paralysis for life.

Sister Kenny believed the irons inhibited recovery and proved a thousand times over that the muscles could be re-educated so that the child could walk again. However, Sister Kenny wasn't a doctor; she was merely a nurse. How dare she dabble in a province that was confined to qualified doctors? It didn't seem to matter that Sister Kenny had found the solution to the problem and had proved her solution to be effective. The children Sister Kenny treated knew she was right, as did their parents, yet the established medical profession not only refused to adopt her methods, it actually prevented her from practicing. It took twenty years before the medical profession would accept what Sister Kenny saw as obvious.

I first saw that film years before I discovered EASYWAY. No doubt there was an element of truth in it. However, it seemed obvious to me that Hollywood had used a large portion of poetic license. Sister Kenny couldn't possibly have discovered something that the combined knowledge of medical science had failed to discover. Surely the established medical specialists weren't the dinosaurs they appeared to be in the film. How could it possibly have taken them twenty years to accept the evidence that was staring them in the face?

They say that fact is stranger than fiction. I apologize for accusing the makers of *Sister Kenny* of using poetic license. Even in this so-called enlightened age of modern communication, after twenty years, I've failed to get my message across. Oh, I've proved my point: you are probably reading this book because another ex-smoker has recommended it to you. Remember, I don't have the massive financial power of institutions like the American Medical Association or the American Lung Association. Like Sister Kenny, I'm a lone individual. Like her, I'm only famous because my system works. I'm already regarded as the number-one guru helping smokers to quit. Like Sister Kenny, I've proved my point. But what good did it do Sister Kenny if the rest of the world was still adopting procedures completely counterproductive to recovery from polio?

As I wrote at the end of the original manuscript: "There is a wind of change in society. A snowball has started that I hope this book will help turn into an avalanche."

From my remarks above, you might have drawn the conclusion that I don't respect the medical profession. Nothing could be further from the truth. One of my sons is a doctor and I know of no finer profession. Indeed, we receive more recommendations to our clinics from doctors than from any other source, and surprisingly, more of our clients come from the medical profession than any other single profession.

In the early years, doctors generally regarded me as being somewhere between a charlatan and a quack. In August 1997, I had the great privilege to be invited to lecture to the 10th World Conference on Tobacco or Health held in Beijing. I believe that I am the first non-physician to receive such an honor. The invitation itself is a measure of the progress that I have made.

However, I might just as well have been lecturing to a brick wall. Since nicotine gum and the patch have failed to cure the problem, smokers themselves appear to have accepted that drug addiction can't be cured by prescribing the same drug. It's equivalent to telling a heroin addict: don't smoke heroin, smoking it is dangerous, try injecting it into your vein (don't try this with nicotine—it will kill you instantly). The medical profession and the media haven't a clue about helping smokers quit; they concentrate on telling smokers what they already know: smoking is unhealthy, it's filthy and disgusting, it's antisocial and expensive. It never seems to occur to them that smokers do not smoke because they don't understand the reasons that they shouldn't smoke. The real solution is to remove the reasons why they do smoke.

On national no-smoking days, the medical experts say something like: "This is the day that every smoker tries to quit!" Every smoker knows that it is the one day in the year that most smokers will smoke twice as many cigarettes as they usually do and twice as blatantly. Smokers don't like being told what to do, particularly by people who don't understand why they smoke and dismiss smokers as mere idiots.

Medical experts who don't completely understand smokers themselves or how to make it easy for smokers to quit suggest: "Try this method. If it doesn't work try another." Imagine ten different ways of treating appendicitis. Nine methods cured ten percent of the patients and killed ninety percent, and the tenth method cured ninety-five percent. Imagine that knowledge of the tenth method had been available for more than twenty years, but the vast majority of the medical profession still recommended the other nine.

One of the doctors at the Beijing conference raised a pertinent point that hadn't occurred to me. He said that doctors might well find themselves liable to a legal action for malpractice, by not advising their patients of the best way to quit smoking. Ironically, he was a great advocate of nicotine replacement therapy (nicotine gums, patches, etc.). I try hard not to be vindictive, but I hope he becomes the first victim of his suggestion.

The British government has wasted millions of pounds on shock TV campaigns trying to persuade younger people not to get hooked. It might just as well have wasted the money trying to persuade them that motorbikes can kill. Youngsters know that one cigarette won't kill them. No one ever expects to get hooked. The link between smoking and lung cancer has been established for more than fifty years. Yet more kids are becoming hooked nowadays than ever before. Kids don't need to watch smoking horrors on TV to witness the actual devastation that smoking causes. I watched my father and my sister destroyed by the weed, but that didn't prevent me from falling into the trap.

I appeared on a national TV show with a doctor from the European Medical Association on Smoking or Health who had never smoked in her life nor cured a single smoker, yet categorically informed the nation about how the Association's campaign would prevent youngsters from becoming hooked. If only the government had had the common sense to give those millions of pounds to me. I could have financed a campaign that would have guaranteed the death of nicotine addiction within a few years.

I truly believe that the snowball has become the size of a soccer ball. But after twenty years, that is still a spit in the ocean. I'm grateful to the thousands of ex-smokers who have visited my clinics, read my books, watched my videos, and recommended EASYWAY to friends, relatives, and anyone who will listen, and I pray that you continue to do so. However, the snowball won't become an avalanche until the medical profession and the media stop recommending methods that make it harder to quit and accept that EASYWAY is not just another method, BUT THE ONLY SENSIBLE METHOD TO USE!

I don't expect you to believe me at this stage, but by the time you have finished this book, you will understand. Even the comparatively few smokers we have failed say something like: "I haven't succeeded yet, but your way is better than any I know."

If when you finish this book you feel that you owe me a debt of gratitude, you can more than repay that debt. Not just by recommending EASYWAY to your friends, but whenever you see a TV or radio show, or read a newspaper article advocating some other method, by writing to or calling them to ask why they aren't advocating EASYWAY. That will start the avalanche, and if I live to witness it, I will die a happy man.

This new edition of EASYWAY gives you the state-of-the-art technology on just how easy and enjoyable it is to quit smoking. Do you have a feeling of doom and gloom? Forget it. I've achieved some marvelous things in my life. By far the greatest was to escape from the slavery of nicotine addiction. I escaped more than twenty years ago and still cannot get over the joy of being free. There is no need to feel depressed—nothing bad is happening. On the contrary, you are about to achieve something that every smoker on the planet would love to achieve: TO BE FREE!

CHAPTER 1

The Worst Nicotine Addict
I Have Yet to Meet

—◀○▶—

Perhaps I should begin by describing my credentials for writing this book. I am not a doctor or a psychiatrist; my qualifications are far more appropriate. I spent thirty-three years of my life as a confirmed smoker. In the latter years I smoked a hundred a day on a bad day, and never fewer than sixty.

I made dozens of attempts to stop. I once quit for six months, and I was still climbing up the wall, still standing near smokers trying to get a whiff of the tobacco, still traveling in the smokers' cars on trains.

With most smokers, on the health side, it's a question of "I'll stop before it happens to me." I had reached the stage where I knew it was killing me. I had a permanent headache from the pressure of the constant coughing. I could feel the continuous throbbing in the vein that runs vertically down the center of my forehead, and I honestly believed that any moment there would be an explosion in my head and I would die from a brain hemorrhage. It bothered me, but it still didn't stop me.

I had reached the stage where I gave up even trying to stop. It was not so much that I enjoyed smoking. Sometime in their lives most smokers suffer from the illusion that they enjoy the odd cigarette, but I never suffered from that illusion. I have always detested the taste and smell, but I thought a cigarette helped me to relax. It gave me courage and confidence, and I was always miserable when I tried to stop, never being able to visualize an enjoyable life without a cigarette.

Eventually my wife sent me to a hypnotherapist. I must confess that I was completely skeptical, knowing nothing about hypnosis in those days and having visions of a Svengali-type figure with piercing eyes and a waving pendulum. I had all the normal illusions that smokers have about smoking except one—I knew that I wasn't a weak-willed person. I was in control of all other aspects of my life, but cigarettes controlled me. I thought that hypnosis involved the forcing of wills, and although I was not obstructive (like most smokers, I dearly wanted to stop), I thought no one was going to kid me that I didn't need to smoke.

The whole session appeared to be a waste of time. The hypnotherapist tried to make me lift my arms and do various other things. Nothing appeared to be working properly. I didn't lose consciousness. I didn't go into a trance, or at least I didn't think I did, and yet after that session, not only did I stop smoking, but I actually enjoyed the process even during the withdrawal period.

Now, before you go rushing off to see a hypnotherapist, let me make something quite clear. Hypnotherapy is a means of communication. If the wrong message is communicated, you won't stop smoking. I'm loath to criticize the man whom I consulted because I would be dead by now if I hadn't seen him. But it was in spite of him, not because of him. Neither do I wish to appear to be knocking hypnotherapy; on the contrary, I use it as part of my own consultations. It is the power of suggestion and a powerful force that can be used for good or evil. Don't ever consult a hypnotherapist unless he or she has been personally recommended by someone you respect and trust.

During those awful years as a smoker I thought that my life depended on cigarettes, and I was prepared to die rather than be without them. Today people ask me whether I ever have the odd pang. The answer is, "Never, never, never"— just the reverse. I've had a wonderful life. If I had died from smoking, I couldn't have complained. I have been a very lucky man, but the most marvelous thing that has ever happened to me is being freed from that nightmare, that slavery of having to go through life systematically destroying my own body and paying through the nose for the privilege.

I am not a mystical figure. I do not believe in magicians or fairies. I have a scientific brain, and I couldn't understand what appeared to me like magic. I started reading up on hypnosis and on smoking. Nothing I read seemed to explain the miracle that had happened. Why had it been so ridiculously easy to stop, whereas previously it had been weeks of black depression?

It took me a long time to work it all out, basically because I was going about it back to front. I was trying to work out why it had been so easy to stop, whereas the real problem is trying to explain why smokers find it *difficult* to stop. Smokers talk about the terrible withdrawal pangs, but when I looked back and tried to remember those awful pangs, they didn't exist for me. There was no physical pain. It was all in the mind.

Now my full-time profession is helping other people to kick the habit. I'm very, very successful. I have helped to cure thousands of smokers. Let me emphasize from the start: there is no such thing as a confirmed smoker. I have still not met anybody who was as badly hooked (or, rather, *thought* he was as badly hooked) as I was. It is basically fear that keeps us smoking: the fear that life will never be quite as enjoyable without cigarettes and the fear of feeling deprived. In fact, nothing could be further from the truth. Not only is life just as enjoyable without them, but also infinitely more so in many ways, and extra health, energy, and wealth are the least of the advantages.

All smokers can find it easy to stop smoking—even you! All you have to do is read the rest of this book with an open mind. The more you can understand, the easier you will find it to stop. Even if you do not understand a word, provided you follow the instructions, you will find stopping easy. Most important of all, you will not go through life moping for cigarettes or feeling deprived. The only mystery will be why you smoked for so long.

Let me issue a warning. There are only two reasons for failure with my method:

1. FAILURE TO CARRY OUT INSTRUCTIONS

   Some people find it annoying that I am so dogmatic about certain recommendations. For example, I will tell you not to try cutting down or using substitutes like sweets or chewing gum (particularly anything containing nicotine). The reason why I am so dogmatic is that I know my subject. I do not deny that there are many people who have succeeded in stopping by using such ruses, but they have succeeded in spite of, not because of them. There are people who can make love standing on a hammock, but it is not the easiest way. Everything I tell you has a purpose: to make it easy to stop and thereby ensure success.

2. FAILURE TO UNDERSTAND

   Do not take anything for granted. Question not only what I tell you, but also your own views and what society has taught you about smoking. For example, those of you who think it is just a habit, ask yourselves why other habits, some of them enjoyable ones, are easy to break, yet a habit that tastes awful, costs us a fortune, and kills us is so difficult to break.

If you think you enjoy a cigarette, ask yourself why other things in life that are infinitely more enjoyable you can take or leave. Why do you have to *have* the cigarette, and why does panic set in if you don't?

CHAPTER 2

The Easy Method

━◀◯▶━

The object of this book is to get you into the frame of mind in which, instead of feeling like you are climbing Mount Everest and spending the next few weeks craving a cigarette and envying other smokers, you start right away with a feeling of elation, as if you had been cured of a terrible disease. From then on, the further you go through life, the more you will look at cigarettes and wonder how you ever smoked them in the first place. You will look at smokers with pity as opposed to envy.

Provided that you are not a non-smoker or an ex-smoker, it is essential to keep smoking until you have finished the book completely. This may appear to be a contradiction. Later I will explain that cigarettes do absolutely nothing for you at all. In fact, one of the many conundrums about smoking is that when we are actually smoking a cigarette, we look at it and wonder why we are doing it. It is only when we are deprived that the cigarette becomes precious. However, let us accept that, whether you like it or not, you believe you are hooked. When you believe you are hooked, you can never be completely relaxed or concentrate properly unless you are smoking. So do not attempt to stop smoking before you have finished the whole book. As you read further your desire to smoke will gradually be reduced. Do not go off half-cocked; this could be fatal. Remember, all you have to do is follow the instructions.

With the benefit of almost twenty years' feedback since the book's original publication, this instruction to continue to smoke until you have completed the book has caused me more frustration than any other. When I first stopped smoking, many of my relatives and friends stopped, purely because I had done it. They thought, "If he can do it, anybody can." Over the years, by dropping little hints I managed to persuade the ones that hadn't stopped to realize just how nice it is to be free! When the book was first printed I gave copies to the hard core who were still puffing away. I worked on the basis that, even if it were the most boring book ever written, they would still read it, if only because it had been written by a friend. I was surprised and hurt to learn that, months later, they hadn't bothered to finish the book. I even discovered that someone who was then my closest friend had not only ignored the original copy I had signed and given to him, but had actually given it away. I was hurt at the time, but I had overlooked the dreadful fear that slavery to the weed instills in the smoker. It can transcend friendship. I nearly provoked a divorce because of it. My mother once said to my wife, "Why don't you threaten to

> ❖
>
> "I know that NOTHING now will make me go back to smoking. It's so nice to be FREE, breathe properly, and not be a slave."
> —CHRISSIE J.
>
> ❖

leave him if he doesn't stop smoking?" My wife said, "Because he'd leave me if I did." I'm ashamed to admit it, but I believe she was right; such is the fear that smoking creates. I now realize that many smokers don't finish the book because they feel they have got to stop smoking when they do. Some deliberately read only one line a day in order to postpone the evil day. Now, I am fully aware that many readers are having their arms twisted by people who love them to read this book. Look at it this way: what have you got to lose? If you don't stop at the end of the book, you are no worse off than you are now. YOU HAVE ABSOLUTELY NOTHING TO LOSE AND SO MUCH TO GAIN!

❖

"I never dreamed I would actually want to give up smoking, let alone have to hold myself back until I had finished the book!"
—RACHEL G.

❖

Incidentally, if you have not smoked for a few days or weeks, but are not sure whether you are a smoker, an ex-smoker, or a non-smoker, then don't smoke while you read. In fact, you are already a non-smoker. All we've now got to do is to let your brain catch up with your body. By the end of the book you'll be a happy non-smoker.

Basically my method is the complete opposite of the normal method of trying to stop. The *normal* method is to list the considerable disadvantages of smoking and say, "If only I can go long enough without a cigarette, eventually the desire to smoke will go. I can then enjoy life again, free of slavery to the weed."

This is the logical way to go about it, and thousands of smokers are stopping every day using variations of this method. However, it is very difficult to succeed using this method for the following reasons:

1. Stopping smoking is not the real problem. Every time you put a cigarette out you stop smoking. You may have powerful reasons on day one to say, "I do not want to smoke any more"—all smokers have, every day of their lives, and the reasons are more powerful than you can possibly imagine. The real problem is day two, day ten, or day ten thousand, when in a weak moment, an inebriated moment, or even a strong moment, you have one cigarette, and then you want another, and suddenly you are a smoker again.

2. The health scares should stop us. Our rational minds say, "Stop doing it. You are a fool," but in fact the health scares make it harder. We smoke, for example, when we are nervous. Tell smokers that cigarettes are killing them, and the first thing they will do is light one. There are more cigarette butts outside the Royal Marsden Hospital, England's foremost cancer treatment establishment, than outside any other hospital in the country.

3. All reasons for stopping actually make it harder for two other reasons. *First,* they create a sense of sacrifice. We are always being forced to give up our little friend or prop or vice or pleasure, whichever way the smoker sees it. *Secondly,* they create a "blind." We do not smoke because we don't understand the reasons we should stop. The real question is "Why do we want or need to do it?"

The Easy Method is basically this: initially to forget the reasons we'd like to stop, to face the cigarette problem, and to ask ourselves the following questions:

1. What is it doing for me?

2. Do I actually enjoy it?

3. Do I really need to go through life paying through the nose just to stick these things in my mouth and suffocate myself?

The beautiful truth is that it does absolutely nothing for you at all. Let me make it quite clear, I do not mean that the disadvantages of being a smoker outweigh the advantages; all smokers know that all their lives. I mean there are not *any* advantages from smoking. The only advantage it ever had was the social "plus"; nowadays even smokers themselves regard it as an antisocial habit.

Most smokers find it necessary to rationalize why they smoke, but the reasons are all fallacies and illusions.

The first thing we are going to do is to remove these fallacies and illusions. In fact, you will realize that there is nothing to give up. Not only is there nothing to give up, but there are also marvelous, positive gains from being a non-smoker, and health and money are only two of these. Once the illusion that life will never be quite as enjoyable without the cigarette is removed, once you realize that not only is life just as enjoyable without it, but infinitely more so, once the feeling of being deprived or of missing out is eradicated, then we can go back to reconsider the health and money—and the dozens of other reasons for stopping smoking. These realizations will become positive additional aids to help you achieve what you really desire—to enjoy the whole of your life free from the slavery of the weed.

CHAPTER 3

Why Is It Difficult to Stop?

—◄◯►—

A s I explained earlier, I got interested in this subject because of my own addiction. When I finally stopped it was like magic. When I had previously tried to stop there were weeks of black depression. There would be odd days when I was comparatively cheerful, but the next day I was depressed again. It was like clawing your way out of a slippery pit: you feel you are near the top, you see the sunshine and then find yourself sliding down again. Eventually you light that cigarette, it tastes awful, and you try to work out why you have to do it.

One of the questions I always ask smokers prior to my consultations is "Do you want to stop smoking?" In a way it is a stupid question. All smokers would love to stop smoking. If you say to the most confirmed smoker, "If you could go back to the time before you became hooked, with the knowledge you have now, would you have started smoking?" "NO WAY" is the reply.

Say to the most confirmed smoker—someone who doesn't think that it injures his health, who is not worried about the social stigma, and who can afford it (there are not many about these days)—"Do you encourage your children to smoke?" "NO WAY" is the reply.

All smokers feel that something evil has got possession of them. In the early days it is a matter of "I am going to stop, not today, but tomorrow." Eventually we get to the stage where we think either that we haven't got the willpower or that there is something inherent to the cigarette that we must have in order to enjoy life.

As I said previously, the problem is not explaining why it is easy to stop; *it is explaining why it is difficult.* In fact, the real problem is explaining why anybody does it in the first place or why, at one time, more than sixty percent of the population in Britain was smoking.

The whole business of smoking is an extraordinary enigma. The only reason we get on to it is because thousands of people are already doing it. Yet every one of them wishes he or she had not started in the first place, telling us that it is a waste of time and money. We cannot quite believe they are not enjoying it. We associate it with being grown-up and work hard to become hooked ourselves. We then spend the rest of our lives telling our own children not to do it and trying to kick the habit ourselves.

We also spend the rest of our lives paying through the nose. The average twenty-a-day smoker spends $100,000 or more in his or her lifetime on cigarettes. What do we do with that money? (It wouldn't be so bad if we just set light to it.) We actually use it systematically to congest our lungs with cancerous tars, progressively to clutter up and poison our blood vessels. Each day we are increasingly starving every muscle and organ of oxygen, so that each day we become more lethargic. We sentence ourselves to a lifetime of filth, bad breath, stained teeth, burnt clothes, filthy ashtrays, and the foul smell of stale tobacco. It is a lifetime of slavery. We spend half our lives in situations in which society forbids us to smoke (churches, hospitals, schools, trains, theaters, and the like) or, when we are trying to cut down or stop, feeling deprived. The rest of our smoking lives is spent in situations where we are allowed to smoke, but wish we didn't have to. What sort of hobby is it that when you are doing it you wish you weren't, and when you are not doing it you crave it? It's a lifetime of being treated by half of society like some sort of leper and, worst of all, a lifetime of an otherwise intelligent, rational human being going through life in self-contempt. The smoker despises himself every National Non-Smoking Day, every time he inadvertently reads the government health warning or there is a cancer scare or a bad-breath campaign, every time he gets congested or has a pain in the chest, every time he is the lone smoker in company with non-smokers. Having to go through life with these awful black shadows at the back of his mind, what does he get out of it? ABSOLUTELY NOTHING!

> ❖
>
> **"I always thought if I quit smoking I would feel less happy and less confident. In fact the beauty of your book is that, from the outset, you FEEL MORE HAPPY AND MORE CONFIDENT!!"**
>
> —JENNIFER O.
>
> ❖

Pleasure? Enjoyment? Relaxation? A prop? A boost? All illusions, unless you consider the wearing of tight shoes to enjoy the removal of them as some sort of pleasure!

As I have said, the real problem is trying to explain not only why smokers find it difficult to stop, but why anybody smokes at all.

You are probably saying, "That's all very well. I know this, but once you are hooked on these things it is very difficult to stop." But why is it so difficult, and why do we have to do it? Smokers search for the answer to these questions all of their lives.

Some say it is because of the powerful withdrawal symptoms. In fact, the actual withdrawal symptoms from nicotine are so mild (see chapter 6) that most smokers have lived and died without ever realizing they are drug addicts.

Some say cigarettes are very enjoyable. They aren't. They are filthy, disgusting objects. Ask any smoker who thinks he smokes only because he enjoys a cigarette if, when he hasn't got his own brand and can only obtain a brand he finds distasteful, he stops smoking. Smokers would rather smoke old rope than not smoke at all. Enjoyment has nothing to do with it. I enjoy lobster but I never got to the stage where I had to have twenty lobsters hanging round my neck. With other things in life, we enjoy them while we are doing them but we don't sit feeling deprived when we are not.

Some search for deep psychological reasons, the "Freudian syndrome," "the child at the mother's breast." Really it is just the reverse. The usual reason why we start smoking is to show we are grown-up and mature. If we had to suck a pacifier in public, we would die of embarrassment.

Some think the appeal is the reverse, the macho effect of breathing smoke or fire down your nostrils. Again this argument has no substance. A burning cigarette in the ear would appear ridiculous. How much more ridiculous to breathe cancer-triggering tars into your lungs.

Some say, "It is something to do with my hands!" So, why light it?

"It is oral satisfaction." So, why light it?

"It is the feeling of the smoke going into my lungs." An awful feeling—it is called suffocation.

Many believe smoking relieves boredom. This is also a fallacy. Boredom is a frame of mind. There is nothing interesting about a cigarette.

For thirty-three years my reason was that it relaxed me, gave me confidence and courage. I also knew it was killing me and costing me a fortune. Why didn't I go to my doctor and ask him for an alternative to relax me and give me courage and confidence?

I didn't go because I knew he would suggest an alternative. It wasn't my reason; it was my excuse.

Some say they only do it because their friends do it. Are they really that stupid? If so, they should pray that their friends do not start cutting their heads off to cure a headache!

Most smokers who think about it eventually come to the conclusion that it is just a habit. This is not really an explanation, but once all the usual rational explanations have been discounted, it appears to be the only remaining excuse. Unfortunately, this explanation is equally illogical. Every day of our lives we change habits, and some of them are very enjoyable. We have been brainwashed into believing that smoking is a habit and that habits are difficult to break. Are habits difficult to break? In the United Kingdom we are in the habit of driving on the left side of the road. Yet when we drive on the European Continent or in the United States, we immediately break that habit with hardly any aggravation whatsoever. It is clearly a fallacy that habits are hard to break. The fact is that we make and break habits every day of our lives.

So why do we find it difficult to break a habit that tastes awful, that kills us, that costs us a fortune, that is filthy and disgusting, and that we would love to break anyway, when all we have to do is to stop doing it? The answer is that smoking is not habit: IT IS NICOTINE ADDICTION!

Most smokers find it difficult to "give up" smoking because they do not understand drug addiction. Their main reason is that they are convinced that they get some genuine pleasure and/or crutch from smoking and believe that they are making a genuine sacrifice if they quit.

The beautiful truth is that once you understand nicotine addiction and the true reasons why you smoke, you will stop doing it—just like that—and within three weeks the only mystery will be why you found it necessary to smoke as long as you did, and why you cannot persuade other smokers HOW NICE IT IS TO BE A NON-SMOKER!

CHAPTER 4

The Sinister Trap

-◄○►-

S moking is the most subtle, sinister trap that man and nature have combined to devise. What gets us into it in the first place? The thousands of adults who are already doing it. They even warn us that it's a filthy, disgusting habit that will eventually destroy us and cost us a fortune, but we cannot believe that they are not enjoying it. One of the many pathetic aspects of smoking is how hard we have to work in order to become hooked.

It is the only trap in nature that has no lure, no piece of cheese. The thing that springs the trap is not that cigarettes taste so good; it's that they taste so awful. If that first cigarette tasted good, alarm bells would ring, and as intelligent human beings, we could then understand why half the adult population was systematically paying through the nose to poison itself. But because that first cigarette tastes awful, our young minds are reassured that we will never become hooked, and we think that because we are not enjoying cigarettes we can stop whenever we want to.

It is the only drug in nature that prevents you from achieving your aim. Boys usually start because they want to appear tough—

like Humphrey Bogart or Clint Eastwood. The last thing you feel with the first cigarette is tough. You dare not inhale, and if you have too many, you start to feel dizzy, then sick. All you want to do is get away from the others and throw the filthy things away.

With women, the aim is often to be sophisticated and modern. We have all seen them taking little puffs on a cigarette, looking absolutely ridiculous. By the time the boys have learned to look tough and the girls have learned to look sophisticated, they wish they had never started in the first place. I wonder whether women ever look sophisticated when they smoke, or whether this is a figment of our imaginations created by cigarette advertisements. It seems to me that there is no intermediary stage between the obvious learner and the veteran smoker.

We then spend the rest of our lives trying to explain to ourselves why we do it, telling our children not to get caught, and at odd times, trying to escape ourselves.

The trap is so designed that we try to stop only when we have stress in our lives, whether it be health, shortage of money, or just plain being made to feel like a leper.

As soon as we stop, we have more stress (the fearful withdrawal pangs of nicotine), and the thing that we rely on to relieve stress (our old prop, the cigarette) we now must do without.

After a few days of torture we decide that we have picked the wrong time. We must wait for a period without stress, and as soon as that arrives the reason for stopping vanishes. Of course, that period will never arrive because, in the first place, we think that our lives tend to become more and more stressful. As we leave the protection of our parents, the natural process is setting up homes, paying mortgages, having babies, working more responsible jobs, and so forth. This is also an illusion. The truth is that the most stressful periods for any creature are early childhood and adolescence. We tend to confuse responsibility with stress. Smokers' lives automatically become more stressful because tobacco does not relax you or relieve stress, as society leads us to believe. Just the reverse: it actually causes you to become more nervous and stressed.

Even those smokers who kick the habit (most do, one or more times during their lives) can lead perfectly happy lives yet suddenly become hooked again.

The whole business of smoking is like wandering into a giant maze. As soon as we enter the maze our minds become misty and clouded, and we spend the rest of our lives trying to escape. Many of us eventually do, only to find that we get trapped again at a later date.

I spent thirty-three years trying to escape from that maze. Like all smokers, I couldn't understand it. However, due to a combination of unusual circumstances, none of which reflect any credit on me, I wanted to know why previously it had been so desperately difficult to stop, and yet, when I finally did, it was not only easy but enjoyable.

Since stopping smoking, my hobby and, later, my profession has been to resolve the many conundrums associated with smoking. It is a complex and fascinating puzzle and, like the Rubik's Cube®, practically impossible to solve. However, like all complicated puzzles, if you know the solution, it is easy! I have the solution to stopping smoking easily. I will lead you out of the maze and ensure that you'll never wander into it again. All you have to do is *follow the instructions*. If you take a wrong turn, the rest of the instructions will be pointless.

Let me emphasize that anybody can find it easy to stop smoking, but first we need to establish the facts. No, I do not mean the scary facts. I know you are already aware of them. There is already enough information on the evils of smoking. If that were going to stop you, you would already have stopped. I mean, why do we find it difficult to stop? In order to answer this question we need to know the real reason why we are still smoking.

CHAPTER 5

Why Do We Carry On Smoking?

—◄○►—

W e all start smoking for stupid reasons, usually social pressures or social occasions, yet once we feel we are becoming hooked, why do we carry on smoking?

No regular smoker knows why he or she smokes. If smokers knew the true reason, they would stop doing it. I have asked the question of thousands of smokers during my consultations. The true answer is the same for all smokers, but the variety of replies is infinite. I find this part of the consultation the most amusing and at the same time the most pathetic.

All smokers know in their heart of hearts that they are fools. They know that they had no need to smoke before they became hooked. Most of them can remember that their first cigarette tasted awful and that they had to work hard in order to become hooked. The most annoying part is that they sense that non-smokers are not missing anything and are laughing at them.

However, smokers are intelligent, rational human beings. They know that they are taking enormous health risks and that they spend a fortune on cigarettes in their lifetime. Therefore it is necessary for them to have a rational explanation to justify their habit.

The actual reason why smokers continue to smoke is a subtle combination of the factors that I will elaborate on in the next two chapters. They are:

1.NICOTINE ADDICTION

2.BRAINWASHING

CHAPTER 6

Nicotine Addiction

—◀○▶—

Nicotine, a colorless, oily compound, is the drug contained in tobacco that addicts the smoker. It is the fastest addictive drug known to mankind, and it can take just one cigarette to become hooked.

Every puff on a cigarette delivers, via the lungs to the brain, a small dose of nicotine that acts more rapidly than the dose of heroin the addict injects into his veins.

If there are twenty puffs for you in a cigarette, you receive twenty doses of the drug with just one cigarette.

Nicotine is a quick-acting drug. Levels in the bloodstream fall quickly to about half within thirty minutes of smoking a cigarette and to a quarter within an hour of finishing a cigarette. This explains why many smokers average about twenty per day.

As soon as the smoker extinguishes the cigarette, the nicotine rapidly starts to leave the body and the smoker begins to suffer withdrawal pangs.

I must at this point dispel a common illusion that smokers have about withdrawal pangs. Smokers think that withdrawal pangs are the terrible trauma they suffer when they try or are forced to stop smoking. These are, in fact, mainly mental; the smoker is feeling deprived of his pleasure or prop. I will explain more about this later.

The actual pangs of withdrawal from nicotine are so subtle that most smokers have lived and died without even realizing they are drug addicts. When we use the term "nicotine addict" we think we just "got into the habit." Most smokers have a horror of drugs, yet that's exactly what they are—drug addicts. Fortunately, it is an easy drug to kick, but you need first to accept that you are addicted.

There is no physical pain in the withdrawal from nicotine. It is merely an empty, restless feeling, the feeling of something missing, which is why many smokers think it is something to do with their hands. If it is prolonged, the smoker becomes nervous, insecure, agitated, lacking in confidence, and irritable. It is like hunger—for a poison, NICOTINE.

Within seven seconds of lighting a cigarette the smoker is supplied with fresh nicotine and the craving ends, resulting in the feeling of relaxation and confidence that the cigarette gives.

In the early days, when we first start smoking, the withdrawal pangs and their relief are so slight that we are not even aware that they exist. When we begin to smoke regularly we think it is because we've either come to enjoy cigarettes or gotten into the "habit." The truth is we're already hooked; we do not realize it, but that little nicotine monster is already inside our stomach and every now and again we have to feed it.

All smokers start smoking for stupid reasons. Nobody has to. The only reason why anybody continues smoking, whether he be a casual or a heavy smoker, is to feed that little monster.

The whole business of smoking is a series of conundrums. All smokers know at heart that they are fools and have been trapped by something evil. However, I think the most pathetic aspect about smoking is that the enjoyment that the smoker gets from a cigarette is the pleasure of trying to get back to the state of peace, tranquility, and confidence that his body had before he became hooked in the first place.

You know that feeling when a neighbor's burglar alarm has been ringing all day, or there has been some other minor, persistent aggravation. Then the noise suddenly stops—that marvelous feeling of peace and tranquility is experienced. It is not really peace but the ending of the aggravation.

Before we start the nicotine chain, our bodies are complete. We then force nicotine into the body, and when we put that cigarette out and the nicotine starts to leave, we suffer withdrawal pangs—not physical pain, but an empty feeling. We are not even aware that it exists, but it is like a dripping tap inside our bodies. Our rational minds do not understand it. They

❖

"Thank you for your insight, your humor; you have thought of every scenario. I laughed out loud many times."
—MRS. J. SANDERS

❖

do not need to. All we know is that we want a cigarette, and when we light one the craving goes, and for the moment we are content and confident again just as we were before we became addicted. However, the satisfaction is only temporary because, in order to relieve the craving, you have to put more nicotine into the body. As soon as you extinguish that cigarette the craving starts again, and so the chain goes on. It is a chain for life—UNLESS YOU BREAK IT.

The whole business of smoking is like wearing tight shoes just to obtain the pleasure you feel when you take them off. There are three main reasons why smokers cannot see things that way.

1. From birth we have been subjected to massive brainwashing telling us that smokers receive immense pleasure and/or

a crutch from smoking. Why should we not believe this? Why else would smokers waste all that money and take such horrendous risks?

2. Because the physical withdrawal from nicotine involves no actual pain but is merely an empty, insecure feeling inseparable from hunger or normal stress, and because those are the very times that we tend to light up, we tend to regard the feeling as normal.

3. However, the main reason that smokers fail to see smoking in its true light is that it works back to front. It's when you are not smoking that you suffer that empty feeling, but because the process of getting hooked is very subtle and gradual in the early days, we regard that feeling as normal and don't blame it on the previous cigarette. The moment you light up, you get an almost immediate boost or buzz and do actually feel less nervous or more relaxed, and the cigarette gets the credit.

It is this reverse process that makes all drugs difficult to kick. Picture the panic state of a heroin addict who has no heroin. Now picture the utter joy when that addict can finally plunge a hypodermic needle into his vein. Can you visualize someone actually getting pleasure by injecting him or herself, or does the mere thought fill you with horror? Non-heroin addicts don't suffer that panic feeling. The heroin doesn't relieve it. On the contrary, it causes it. Non-smokers don't suffer the empty feeling of needing a cigarette or start to panic when the supply runs out. Non-smokers cannot understand how smokers can possibly obtain pleasure from sticking those filthy things in their mouths, setting light to them, and actually inhaling the filth into their lungs. And do you know something? Smokers cannot understand why they do it either.

We talk about smoking being relaxing or giving satisfaction. But how can you be satisfied unless you were dissatisfied in the first place? Why don't non-smokers suffer from this dissatisfied state, and why, after a meal, when non-smokers are completely relaxed, are smokers completely unrelaxed until they have satisfied that little nicotine monster?

Forgive me if I dwell on this subject for a moment. The main reason that smokers find it difficult to quit is that they believe that they are giving up a genuine pleasure or crutch. It is absolutely essential to understand that you are giving up nothing whatsoever.

The best way to understand the subtleties of the nicotine trap is to compare it with eating. If we are in the habit of eating regular meals, we are not aware of being hungry between meals. Only if the meal is delayed are we aware of being hungry, and even then, there is no physical pain, just that empty, insecure feeling we know as: "I need to eat." And the process of satisfying our hunger is a very pleasant pastime.

Smoking appears to be almost identical. That empty, insecure feeling we know as "wanting or needing a cigarette" is identical to a hunger for food, although one will not satisfy the other. Like hunger, there is no physical pain and the feeling is so imperceptible that we are not even aware of it between cigarettes. It's only if we want to light up and aren't allowed to do so that we become aware of any discomfort. But when we do light up we feel satisfied.

It is this similarity to eating that helps fool smokers into believing that they receive some genuine pleasure. Some smokers find it very difficult to grasp that there is no pleasure or crutch whatsoever to smoking. Some argue: "How can you say there is no crutch? You tell me when I light up that I'll feel less nervous than before."

Although eating and smoking appear to be very similar, they are in fact exact opposites:

1. We eat to survive and to prolong our lives, whereas smoking shortens our lives.

2. Food genuinely tastes good, and eating is a genuinely pleasant experience that we enjoy throughout our lives, whereas smoking involves breathing foul and poisonous fumes into our lungs.

3. Eating doesn't create hunger and genuinely relieves it, whereas the first cigarette starts the craving for nicotine, and each subsequent one, far from relieving it, ensures that you continue to suffer that craving for the rest of your life.

This is an opportune moment to dispel another common myth about smoking—that smoking is a habit. Is eating a habit? If you think so, try breaking it completely. No, to describe eating as a habit would be the same as describing breathing as a habit. Both are essential for survival. It is true that different people are in the habit of satisfying their hunger at different times and with varying types of food. But eating itself is not a habit. Neither is smoking. The only reason any smoker lights a cigarette is to try to end the empty, insecure feeling that the previous cigarette created. It is true that different smokers are in the habit of trying to relieve their withdrawal pangs at different times, but smoking itself is not a habit.

Society frequently refers to the smoking habit and in this book, for convenience, I also refer to the "habit." However, be constantly aware that smoking is not habit; it is DRUG ADDICTION!

When we start to smoke we have to force ourselves to learn to cope with it. Before we know it, we are not only buying cigarettes regularly but we *have* to have them. If we don't, panic sets in, and as we go through life we tend to smoke more and more.

This is because, as with any other drug, the body tends to become immune to the effects of nicotine and our intake tends to increase. After quite a short period of smoking, the cigarette ceases to relieve completely the withdrawal pangs that it creates, so that when you light up a cigarette you feel better than you did a moment before, but you are in fact more nervous and less re-laxed than you would be as a non-smoker, even when you are ac-tually smoking the cigarette. The practice is even more ridiculous than wearing tight shoes because as you go through life an in-creasing amount of the discomfort remains even when the shoes are removed.

The position is even worse because, once the cigarette is extin-guished, the nicotine rapidly begins to leave the body, which ex-plains why, in stressful situations, the smoker tends to chain-smoke.

As I have said, the "habit" doesn't exist. The real reason why every smoker goes on smoking is because of that little monster inside his stomach. Every now and again he has to feed it. The smoker himself will decide when he does that, and it tends to be on four types of occasions or a combination of them.

They are:

BOREDOM/CONCENTRATION—two complete opposites!
STRESS/RELAXATION—two complete opposites!

What magic drug can suddenly reverse the very effect it had twenty minutes before? If you think about it, what other types of occasions are there in our lives, apart from sleep? The truth is that smoking neither relieves boredom and stress nor promotes con-centration and relaxation. It is all just illusion.

Apart from being a drug, nicotine is also a powerful poison and is used in insecticides (look it up in your dictionary). The nicotine content of just one cigarette, if injected directly into a vein, would kill you. In fact, tobacco contains many poisons, in-cluding carbon monoxide, and the tobacco plant belongs to the same family as deadly nightshade.

In case you have visions of switching to a pipe or to cigars, I should make it quite clear that the content of this book applies to all tobacco and any substance that contains nicotine, including gum, patches, nasal sprays, and inhalators.

The human body is the most sophisticated object on our planet. No species, even the lowest amoeba or worm, can survive without knowing the difference between food and poison.

Through a process of natural selection over thousands of years, our minds and bodies have developed techniques for distinguishing between food and poison and fail-safe methods for ejecting the latter.

All human beings are averse to the smell and taste of tobacco until they become hooked. If you blow diluted tobacco into the face of any animal or child before it becomes hooked, it will cough and splutter.

When we smoked that first cigarette, inhaling resulted in a coughing fit, or if we smoked too many the first time, we experienced a dizzy feeling or actual physical sickness. It was our body telling us, "YOU ARE FEEDING ME POISON. STOP DOING IT." This is the stage that often determines whether we become smokers or not. It is a fallacy that physically weak and mentally weak people become smokers. The lucky ones are those who find that first cigarette repulsive; physically their lungs cannot cope with it, and they are cured for life. Or, alternatively, they are not mentally prepared to go through the severe learning process of trying to inhale without coughing.

To me, how hard we worked to become hooked is the most tragic part of this whole business, and this is why it is difficult to stop teenagers. Because they are still learning to smoke, because they still find cigarettes distasteful, they believe they can stop whenever they want to. Why do they not learn from us? Then again, why did we not learn from our parents?

Many smokers believe they enjoy the taste and smell of the tobacco. It is an illusion. What we are actually doing when we learn to smoke is teaching our bodies to become immune to the bad smell and taste in order to get our fix, like heroin addicts who think that they enjoy injecting themselves. The withdrawal pangs from heroin are relatively severe, and all they are really enjoying is the ritual of relieving those pangs.

The smoker teaches himself to shut his mind to the bad taste and smell to get his "fix." Ask a smoker who believes he smokes only because he enjoys the taste and smell of tobacco, "If you cannot get your normal brand of cigarette and can only obtain a brand you find distasteful, do you stop smoking?" No way. A smoker will smoke old rope rather than abstain, and it doesn't matter if you switch to mentholated cigarettes, cigars, or a pipe; they taste awful, but if you persevere you will learn to like them. Smokers will even try to keep smoking during colds, flu, sore throats, bronchitis, and emphysema.

Enjoyment has nothing to do with it. If it did, no one would smoke more than one cigarette. There are even thousands of ex-smokers hooked on that filthy nicotine chewing gum that doctors prescribe, and many of them are still smoking.

During my consultations some smokers find it alarming to realize they are drug addicts and think it will make it even more difficult to stop. In fact, it is all good news for two important reasons:

1. The reason why most of us carry on smoking is that, although we know the disadvantages outweigh the advantages, we believe that there is something in the cigarette that we actually enjoy or that it is some sort of prop. We feel that after we stop smoking there will be a void, that certain situations in our life will never be quite the same. This is an illusion. The fact is the cigarette gives nothing; it only takes away and then partially restores to create the illusion. I will explain this in more detail in a later chapter.

2. Although it is the world's most powerful drug because of the speed in which you become hooked, you are never badly hooked. Because it is a quick-acting drug it takes only three weeks for ninety-nine percent of the nicotine to leave your

body, and the actual withdrawal pangs are so mild that most smokers have lived and died without ever realizing that they have suffered them.

You will quite rightly ask why it is that many smokers find it so difficult to stop, go through months of torture, and spend the rest of their lives pining for a cigarette at odd times. The answer is the second reason why we smoke—the brainwashing. The chemical addiction is easy to cope with.

Most smokers go all night without a cigarette. The withdrawal pangs do not even wake them up.

Many smokers will actually leave the bedroom before they light that first cigarette; many will have breakfast first; many will wait until they arrive at work. They can suffer ten hours' withdrawal pangs, and it doesn't bother them, but if they went ten hours during the day without a cigarette, they'd be tearing their hair out.

Many smokers will buy a new car nowadays and refrain from smoking in it. Many will visit theaters, supermarkets, churches, and the like, and not be bothered by not being able to smoke. Even on the subway trains there have been no riots. Smokers are almost pleased for someone or something to force them to stop smoking.

Nowadays many smokers will automatically refrain from smoking in the home of or in the company of non-smokers with little discomfort to themselves. In fact, most smokers have extended periods during which they abstain without effort. Even in my case I would quite happily relax all evening without a cigarette. In the later years as a smoker I actually used to look forward to the evenings when I could stop choking myself (what a ridiculous "habit").

The chemical addiction is easy to cope with, even when you are still addicted, and there are thousands of smokers who remain casual smokers all their lives. They are just as heavily addicted as the heavy smoker. There are even heavy smokers who have kicked the "habit" but will have an occasional cigar, and that keeps them addicted.

As I say, the actual nicotine addiction is not the main problem. It just acts like a catalyst to keep our minds confused over the real problem: the brainwashing.

It may be of consolation to life-long and heavy smokers to know that it is just as easy for them to stop as it is for casual smokers. In a peculiar way, it is easier. The further you go along with the "habit," the more it drags you down and the greater the gain when you stop.

It may be of further consolation for you to know that the rumors that occasionally circulate (such as, "It takes seven years for the 'gunk' to leave your body" or "Every cigarette you smoke takes five minutes off your life") are untrue.

Do not think the bad effects of smoking are exaggerated. If anything, they are sadly understated. The truth is the five minutes rule is obviously an estimation and applies only if you contract one of the killer diseases or just gunk yourself to a standstill.

❖

"I have not had any nightmares or sleepless nights unlike my last attempt at stopping smoking nor have I felt particularly miserable. Quite the opposite . . . it was like a totally new life that I was in control of."
—MARTHA F.

In fact, the gunk never leaves your body completely. If there are smokers about, the gunk is in the atmosphere, and even non-smokers inhale a small percentage. However, these bodies of ours are incredible machines and have enormous powers of recovery, providing we haven't already triggered off one of the irreversible diseases. If you stop now, your body will recover within a matter of a few weeks, almost as if you had never been a smoker.

As I have said, it is never too late to stop. I have helped cure many smokers in their fifties and sixties and even a few in their seventies and eighties. A ninety-one-year-old woman attended my clinic with her sixty-six-year-old son. When I asked her why she had decided to stop smoking, she replied, "To set an example for him." She contacted me six months later saying she felt like a young girl again.

The further it drags you down, the greater the relief. When I finally stopped I went straight from a hundred a day to ZERO, and didn't have one bad pang. In fact, it was actually enjoyable, even during the withdrawal period.

But we *must* remove the brainwashing.

CHAPTER 7

Brainwashing and the
Sleeping Partner

◄○►

How or why do we start smoking in the first place? To understand this fully you need to examine the powerful effect of the subconscious mind or, as I call it, the "sleeping partner."

We all tend to think we are intelligent, dominant human beings determining our paths through life. In fact, ninety-nine percent of our makeup is molded. We are a product of the society in which we are raised—the sort of clothes we wear, the houses we live in, our basic life patterns, even those matters on which we tend to differ such as politics.

Even in matters of fact rather than opinion millions of people can be deluded. Before Columbus sailed to the Americas, the majority of people knew the world to be flat. Today we know it is round. If I wrote a dozen books trying to persuade you that it was flat, I could not do it, yet how many of us have been into space to see the globe? Even if you have flown or sailed around the world, how do you know that you were not traveling in a circle above a flat surface?

Advertisers know well the power of suggestion over the subconscious mind. You think that ads in magazines are a waste of money? That they do not persuade you to buy cigarettes? You are wrong! Try it out for yourself. Next time you go into a bar or restaurant on a cold day and your companion asks you what you are having to drink, instead of saying, "A brandy" (or whatever), embellish it with "Do you know what I would really enjoy today? That marvelous warm glow of a brandy." You will find that even people who dislike brandy will join you.

From our earliest years our subconscious minds are bombarded daily with messages telling us that cigaretttes are the most precious thing on this earth; they relax us and give us confidence and courage. You think I exaggerate? Whenever you see a cartoon, film, or play in which someone is about to be executed or shot, what is often his last request? That's right, a cigarette. The impact of this does not register on our conscious minds, but the "sleeping partner," our subconscious, has time to absorb it. What the message is really saying is, "The most precious thing on this earth, my last thought and action, will be the smoking of a cigarette." In almost every war film the injured man is given a cigarette.

You think that things have changed recently? No. Our children are still being bombarded by large billboards and magazine advertisements. Cigarette advertising is supposed to be banned on television nowadays, yet during peak viewing hours in Britain the world's top darts players are seen constantly puffing away. The programs are usually sponsored by the tobacco giants, and this is the most sinister trend of all in today's advertising: the link with sporting occasions and the jet set. Grand Prix racing cars are modeled and even named after cigarette brand names—or is it the other way round? I've even seen plugs on television depicting a naked couple sharing a cigarette in bed after having sex. The implications are obvious. How my admiration goes out to the advertisers of the small cigar, not for their motives, but for the brilliance of their campaign, wherein a man is about to face death or disaster—his balloon is on fire and about to crash, or the sidecar of his motorbike is about to crash into a river, or he is Columbus and his ship is about to go over the edge of the world. Not a word is spoken. Soft music plays. He lights up a cigar; a look of sheer bliss covers his face. The conscious mind may not realize that the smoker is even watching the advertisement, but the "sleeping partner" is patiently digesting the obvious implications.

True, there is publicity the other way—the cancer scares, the legs being amputated, the bad-breath campaigns—but these do not actually stop people from smoking. Logically they should, but the fact is they do not. They do not even prevent youngsters from starting. All the years that I remained a smoker I honestly believed that, had I known of the links between lung cancer and cigarette smoking, I would never have become a

❖

"Your instruction of continuing to smoke while reading the book is very clever. As I read, I felt myself being conscious of every cigarette I smoked."
—KIRSTY L.

❖

smoker. The truth is that it doesn't make the slightest bit of difference. The trap is the same today as when Sir Walter Raleigh fell into it. All the anti-smoking campaigns just add to the confusion. Even the products themselves, those lovely shining packs that lure you into trying their contents, contain a deadly warning on their sides. What smoker ever reads it, let alone faces the implications of it?

I believe that a leading cigarette manufacturer is actually using the surgeon general's warning to sell its products. The health warning is now so large and bold that the smoker cannot avoid it, however hard he tries. The pang of fear that the smoker suffers prompts him or her to reach for the glossy pack.

Ironically, the most powerful force in this brainwashing is the smoker himself. It is a fallacy that smokers are weak-willed or physically weak. You have to be physically strong in order to cope with the poison.

This is one of the reasons why smokers refuse to accept the overwhelming statistics that prove that smoking cripples your health. Everyone knows of an Uncle Fred who smoked forty a day, never had a day's illness in his life, and lived to eighty. Smokers refuse even to consider the hundreds of other smokers who are cut down in their prime or the fact that Uncle Fred might still be alive if he hadn't been a smoker.

If you do a small survey among your friends and colleagues, you will find that most smokers are, in fact, strong-willed people. They tend to be self-employed, business executives, or in specialized professions, such as doctors, lawyers, policemen, teachers, salesmen, nurses, secretaries, housewives with children—in other words, anybody leading a stressful existence. The main delusion of smokers is that smoking relieves stress and tends to be associated with the dominant type, the type that takes on responsibility and stress, and, of course, that is the type we admire and therefore tend to copy. Another group that tends to get hooked is people in monotonous jobs, because the other main reason for smoking is boredom. However, the idea that smoking relieves boredom is also an illusion, I am afraid.

The extent of the brainwashing is quite incredible. As a society we get all uptight about glue-sniffing, heroin addiction, and other drug addictions. Actual deaths from glue-sniffing do not amount to one hundred per annum, and deaths from heroin are no more than several hundred a year in England, for example.

There is another drug, nicotine, on which more than sixty percent of us become hooked at some time in our lives and the majority spend the rest of their lives paying for it through the nose. Most of their spare money goes toward cigarettes, and hundreds of thousands of people have their lives ruined every year because they became hooked. It is the number one killer in society.

Why is it that we regard glue-sniffing and heroin addiction as such great evils, while the drug that we spend most of our money on and is actually killing us we, until recently, regarded as a perfectly acceptable social habit? In recent years it has been considered a slightly unsociable habit that may injure our health, but is legal and on sale in glossy packs in newsstands, bars, clubs, and restaurants. The biggest vested interest in Britain is the government. It makes £8 billion per year from smokers, and the tobacco companies spend over £100 million per year in promotion alone.

You need to start building resistance to this brainwashing, just as if you were buying a car from a secondhand dealer. You would be nodding politely, but you would not believe a word the man was saying.

Start looking at the filth and poison beneath the these glossy packs. Do not be fooled by the cut-glass ashtrays, the gold lighter, or the millions who have been conned. Start asking yourself:

> Why am I doing it?
> Do I really need to?
> NO, OF COURSE YOU DON'T.

I find this brainwashing aspect the most difficult of all to explain. Why is it that an otherwise rational, intelligent human being becomes a complete imbecile about his own addiction? It pains me to confess that out of the thousands of people I have assisted in kicking the habit, I was the biggest idiot of all.

Not only did I reach a hundred a day myself, but my father was a heavy smoker. He was a strong man, cut down in his prime due to smoking. I can remember watching him when I was a boy; he would be coughing and spluttering in the mornings. I could see he wasn't enjoying it and it was so obvious to me that something evil had gotten possession of him. I can remember saying to my mother, "Don't ever let me become a smoker."

At the age of fifteen I was a physical-fitness fanatic. Sports were my life and I was full of courage and confidence. If anybody had said to me in those days that I would end up smoking a hundred cigarettes a day, I would have gambled my lifetime's earnings that it would not happen, and I would have given any odds that had been asked.

By the age of forty I was a physical and mental cigarette junkie. I had reached the stage where I couldn't carry out the most mundane physical or mental act without first lighting up. With most smokers the triggers are the normal stresses of life, like answering the telephone or socializing. I couldn't even change a television channel or a lightbulb without lighting up.

I knew it was killing me. There was no way I could kid myself otherwise. But I cannot understand why I couldn't see what it was doing to me mentally. It was almost jumping up and biting me on the nose. The ridiculous thing is that most smokers suffer the delusion at some time in their life that they enjoy a cigarette. I never suffered that delusion. I smoked because I thought it helped me concentrate and because it helped my nerves. Now that I am a non-smoker, the most difficult part is trying to believe that those days actually happened. It's like awakening from a nightmare, and that is about the size of it. Nicotine is a drug, and your senses are drugged—your taste buds, your sense of smell. The worst aspect of smoking isn't the injury to your health or pocket, it is the warping of the mind. You search for any plausible excuse to go on smoking.

I remember at one stage switching to a pipe, after a failed attempt to kick cigarettes, in the belief that it was less harmful and would cut down my intake. Some of those pipe tobaccos are absolutely foul. The aroma can be pleasant, but they are awful to smoke. I can remember that for about three months the tip of my tongue was as sore as a boil. A liquid brown goo collects in the bottom of the pipe bowl. Occasionally you unwittingly bring the bowl above the horizontal and before you realize it you have swallowed a mouthful of the filthy stuff. The result is that you usually throw up immediately, no matter whose company you are in.

It took me three months to learn to cope with the pipe, but what I cannot understand is why I didn't sit down sometime during that three months and ask myself why I was subjecting myself to the torture.

Of course, having learned to cope with the pipe, no one appears more contented than pipe smokers. Most of them are convinced that they smoke because they enjoy the pipe. But why did they have to work so hard to learn to like it when they were perfectly happy without it?

The answer is that once you have become addicted to nicotine, the brainwashing is increased. Your subconscious mind knows that the little monster has to be fed, and you block everything else from your mind. As I have already stated, it is fear that keeps people smoking, the fear of that empty, insecure feeling that comes when you stop supplying the nicotine. Because you are not aware of it doesn't mean it isn't there. You don't have to understand it any more than a cat needs to understand where the under-floor hot-water pipes are. The cat just knows that if it sits in a certain place it gets the feeling of warmth.

It is the brainwashing that is the main difficulty in giving up smoking. The brainwashing of our upbringing in society reinforced with the brainwashing from our own addiction and, most powerful of all, the brainwashing of our friends, relatives, and colleagues.

Did you notice that up to now I've frequently referred to "giving up" smoking. I used the expression at the beginning of the previous paragraph. This is a classic example of the brainwashing. The expression implies a genuine sacrifice. The beautiful truth is that there is absolutely nothing to give up. On the contrary, you will be freeing yourself from a terrible disease and achieving marvelous positive gains. We are going to start removing this brainwashing now. From this point on, no longer will we refer to "giving up," but to stopping, quitting, or the true position: ESCAPING!

The only thing that persuades us to smoke in the first place is all the other people doing it. We feel we are missing out. We work so hard to become hooked, yet nobody ever finds out what he or she has been missing. But every time we see another smoker he reassures us that there must be something in it, otherwise he wouldn't be doing it. Even when he has kicked the habit, the ex-smoker feels he is being deprived when a smoker lights up at a party or other social function. He feels safe. He can have just one. And, before he knows it, he is hooked again.

This brainwashing is very powerful and you need to be aware of its effects. Many older smokers in Britain remember the Paul Temple detective series, a very popular radio show after World War II. One of the episodes dealt with addiction to marijuana. Unbeknownst to the smoker, wicked men were selling cigarettes that contained pot. There were no harmful effects. People merely became addicted and had to go on buying the cigarettes. (During my consultations literally hundreds of smokers have admitted to trying pot. None of them said they became hooked on it.) I was about seven years old when I listened to the program. It was my first knowledge of drug addiction. The concept of addiction, being compelled to go on taking the drug, filled me with horror, and even to this day, in spite of the fact that I am fairly convinced that pot is not addictive, I would not dare take one puff of marijuana.

How ironic that I should have ended up a junkie on the world's number one addictive drug. If only Paul Temple had warned me about the cigarette itself. How ironic, too, that more than sixty years later mankind spends millions on cancer research, yet many millions more are spent persuading healthy teenagers to become hooked on the filthy weed, with government having the largest vested interest.

We are about to remove the brainwashing. It is not the non-smoker who is being deprived but the poor smoker who is forfeiting a lifetime of:

○ HEALTH
○ ENERGY
○ WEALTH
○ PEACE OF MIND
○ CONFIDENCE
○ COURAGE
○ SELF-RESPECT
○ HAPPINESS
○ FREEDOM

And what does the smoker gain from these considerable sacrifices?

ABSOLUTELY NOTHING—except the illusion of trying to get back to the state of peace, tranquility, and confidence that the non-smoker enjoys all the time.

CHAPTER 8

Relieving Withdrawal Pangs

—◄o►—

A s I explained earlier, smokers think they smoke for enjoyment, relaxation, or some sort of boost. In fact, this is
an illusion. The actual reason is the relief of withdrawal pangs.

In the early days we use the cigarette as a social prop. We can
take it or leave it. However, the subtle chain has started. Our subconscious mind begins to learn that a cigarette taken at certain
times tends to be pleasurable.

As you become hooked on the drug, the need to relieve the
withdrawal pangs increases. The further the cigarette drags you
down, the more you are fooled into believing it is doing the opposite. It all happens so slowly, so gradually, you are not even
aware of it. Each day you feel no different from the day before.
Most smokers don't even realize they are hooked until they actually try to stop, and even then many won't admit to it. A few stal-
warts just keep their heads in the sand all their lives, trying to
convince themselves and other people that they enjoy it.

I have had the following conversation with hundreds
of teenagers:

ME: *You realize that nicotine is a drug and that the only reason why you are smoking is that you cannot stop.*

T: *Nonsense! I enjoy it. If I didn't, I would stop.*

ME: *Just stop for a week to prove to me you can if you want to.*

T: *No need. I enjoy it. If I wanted to stop, I would.*

ME: *Just stop for a week to prove to yourself you are not hooked.*

T: *What's the point? I enjoy it.*

As already stated, smokers tend to relieve their withdrawal pangs at times of stress, boredom, concentration, relaxation, or a combination of these. This point is explained in greater detail in the next few chapters.

CHAPTER 9

Stress

—◀○▶—

I am referring not only to the great tragedies of life but also to the minor stresses—the socializing, the telephone calls, the anxieties of the parent with noisy young children, and so on.

Let us use the telephone conversation as an example. For most people the telephone is slightly stressful, particularly for people in business. Most calls aren't from satisfied customers or your boss congratulating you. There's usually some sort of aggravation—something going wrong or somebody making demands. At that time the smoker, if not already doing so, will light up a cigarette. The smoker doesn't know or think about why he does this, but for some reason it appears to help.

What has actually happened is this: without being conscious of it, the smoker has already been suffering aggravation (the withdrawal pangs). By partially relieving that aggravation at the same time as normal stress, the total stress is reduced and the smoker gets a boost. At this point the boost is not, in fact, an illusion. The smoker will feel better than before lighting the cigarette. However, even when smoking that cigarette the smoker is more tense than the non-smoker because the more you get into the drug, the more it knocks you down and the less it restores you when you smoke.

I promised no shock treatment. In the example I am about to give, I am not trying to shock you; I am merely emphasizing that cigarettes destroy your nerves rather than relax them.

Try to imagine getting to the stage where a doctor tells you that unless you stop smoking he is going to have to remove your legs. Just for a moment pause and try to visualize life without your legs. Try to imagine the frame of mind of a man who, issued that warning, actually continues smoking and then has his legs removed.

I used to hear stories like that and then would dismiss them as nonsense. In fact, I used to wish a doctor would tell me that; then I would have stopped. Yet I was already fully expecting any day to have a brain hemorrhage and lose not only my legs, but also my life. I didn't think of myself as crazy, just a heavy smoker.

Such stories are not nonsense. That is what this awful drug does to you. As you go through life it systematically takes away your nerve and courage. The more it takes your courage away, the more you are deluded into believing the cigarette is doing the opposite. We have all heard of the panic that overtakes smokers when they are out late at night and in fear of running out of cigarettes. Non-smokers do not suffer from this. The cigarette causes the feeling. At the same time, as you go through life the cigarette not only destroys your nerves, but is also a powerful poison, progressively

❖

"If every smoker could read this book with an open mind, tobacco companies would cease to exist, and there would be millions of very, very happy people."
—CAROLE ANNE F.

❖

destroying your physical health. By the time the smoker reaches the stage at which it is life-threatening, he or she believes the cigarette offers courage and cannot face life without it.

Get it clear in your head that the cigarette is not relieving your nerves; it is slowly but steadily destroying them. One of the great gains of breaking the habit is the return of your confidence and self-assurance.

CHAPTER 10

Boredom

——◀◯▶——

If you are already smoking at this moment, you had probably already forgotten about it until I reminded you.

Another fallacy about smoking is that cigarettes relieve boredom. Boredom is a frame of mind. When you smoke a cigarette your mind isn't saying, "I'm smoking a cigarette. I'm smoking a cigarette." The only time that happens is when you have been deprived for a long time or are trying to cut down, or during those first few cigarettes after a failed attempt to stop.

The true situation is this: when you are addicted to nicotine and are not smoking, there is something missing. If you have something to occupy your mind that isn't stressful, you can go for long periods without being bothered by the absence of the drug. However, when you are bored there's nothing to take your mind off it, so you feed the monster. When you are indulging yourself (that is, not trying to stop or cut down), even lighting up becomes subconscious. Even pipe smokers and roll-your-own smokers can perform this ritual automatically. If any smoker tries to remember the cigarettes he has smoked during the day, he can remember only a small proportion of them—the first one of the day or the one after a meal.

The truth is that cigarettes tend to increase boredom indirectly because they make you feel lethargic. Instead of undertaking some energetic activity smokers tend to lounge around, bored, relieving their withdrawal pangs.

This is why countering the brainwashing is so important. Smokers tend to smoke when bored, and because we've been told since birth that smoking relieves boredom, it doesn't occur to us to question the fact. We've also been brainwashed into believing that chewing gum aids relaxation. It is a fact that when under stress people tend to grind their teeth. All chewing gum does is to give you a logical reason to grind your teeth. Next time you watch someone chewing gum, observe him or her closely and ask yourself whether that person looks relaxed or tense. Observe smokers who are smoking because they are bored. They still looked bored. The cigarette doesn't relieve the boredom.

> ❖
>
> "I met a representative for Nicorette and he said, 'You always know Allen Carr ex-smokers because they are all happy ex-smokers.'"
> —UNA M.
>
> ❖

As an ex-chain-smoker I can assure you that there are no more boring activities in life than lighting up one filthy cigarette after another, day in, day out, year in, year out.

CHAPTER 11

Concentration

—◄○►—

Cigarettes do not help concentration. That is just another illusion.

When you are trying to concentrate, you automatically try to avoid distractions such as feeling cold or hot. The smoker is already suffering: that little monster wants his fix. So when the smoker wants to concentrate he doesn't even have to think about it. He automatically lights up, partially ends the craving, gets on with the matter at hand, and has already forgotten that he is smoking.

Cigarettes do not help concentration. They help to ruin it because after a while, even while smoking a cigarette, the smoker's withdrawal pangs cease to be completely relieved. The smoker then increases his intake, thus increasing the problem.

Concentration is also affected adversely for another reason. The progressive blocking of the arteries and veins with poisons starves the brain of oxygen. In fact, concentration and inspiration are greatly improved as this process is reversed.

It was the concentration aspect that prevented me from succeeding when using the Willpower Method. I could put up with the irritability and bad temper, but when I really needed to concentrate on something difficult, I had to have that cigarette. I can well remember the panic I felt when I discovered that I was not allowed to smoke during my accounting exams. I was already a chain-smoker and convinced that I would not be able to concentrate for three hours without a cigarette. But I passed the exams, and I can't even remember thinking about smoking at the time. So, when it came to the crunch, it obviously didn't bother me.

The loss of concentration that smokers suffer when they try to stop smoking is not, in fact, due to the physical withdrawal from nicotine. When you are a smoker, you have mental blocks. When you have one, what do you do? If you are not already smoking a cigarette, you light up. That doesn't cure the mental block, so then what do you do? You do what you have to do: you get on with it, just as non-smokers do. When you are a smoker nothing gets blamed on the cigarette. Smokers never have smoking coughs; they just have permanent colds. The moment you stop smoking, everything that goes wrong in your life is blamed on the fact that you've stopped smoking. Now when you have a mental block, instead of just getting on with it you start to say, "If only I could light up now, it would solve my problem." You then start to question your decision to quit smoking.

If you believe that smoking is a genuine aid to concentration, then worrying about it will guarantee that you won't be able to concentrate. It's the doubting, not the physical withdrawal pangs, that causes the problem. Always remember: it is smokers who suffer withdrawal pangs, not non-smokers.

When I extinguished my last cigarette I went overnight from a hundred a day to zero without any apparent loss of concentration.

Chapter 12

Relaxation

—◄○►—

Most smokers think that a cigarette helps them relax. The truth is that nicotine is a chemical stimulant. If you take your pulse and then smoke two consecutive cigarettes, there will be a marked increase in your pulse rate.

One of the favorite cigarettes for most smokers is the one after a meal. A meal is a time of day when we stop working. We sit down and relax, relieve our hunger and thirst, and are then completely satisfied. However, the poor smoker cannot relax, as he has another hunger to satisfy. He thinks of the cigarette as the icing on the cake, but it is the little monster that needs feeding.

The truth is that the nicotine addict can never be completely relaxed, and as you go through life it gets worse.

The most unrelaxed people on this planet aren't non-smokers, but fifty-year-old business executives who chain-smoke, are permanently coughing and spluttering, have high blood pressure, and are constantly irritable. At this point cigarettes cease to relieve even partially the symptoms that they have created.

I can remember when I was a young accountant, bringing up a family. One of my children would do something wrong, and I would lose my temper to an extent that was out of all proportion to what he had done. I really believed that I had an evil demon in my makeup. I now know that I did; however it wasn't some inherent flaw in my character, but the little nicotine monster that was creating the problem. During those times I thought I had all the problems in the world, but when I look back on my life, I wonder where all the great stress was. In every other area in my life I was in control. The one thing that controlled me was the cigarette. The sad thing is that even today I can't convince my children that it was the smoking that caused me to be so irritable. Every time they hear a smoker trying to justify his addiction, the message is "Oh, cigarettes calm me. They help me to relax."

Several years ago, the adoption authorities in the UK threatened to prevent smokers from adopting children. A man rang up, irate. He said, "You are completely wrong. I can remember when I was a child—if I had a contentious matter to raise with my mother, I would wait until she lit a cigarette because she was more relaxed then." Why couldn't he talk to his mother when she wasn't smoking a cigarette? Why are smokers so unrelaxed when they are not smoking, even after a meal at a restaurant? Why are nonsmokers completely relaxed then? Why are smokers unable to relax without a cigarette? Start watching them, particularly when they aren't allowed to smoke. You'll find that they have their hands near their mouths, or they are twiddling their thumbs, or tapping their feet, or fiddling with their hair, or clenching their jaw. Smokers aren't relaxed. They've forgotten what it feels like to be completely relaxed. That's one of the many joys you have to come.

The whole business of smoking can be likened to a fly being caught in a pitcher plant. To begin with, the fly is eating the nectar. At some imperceptible stage the plant begins to eat the fly.

Isn't it time you climbed out of that plant?

CHAPTER 13

Combination Cigarettes

—◀◦▶—

N o, a combination cigarette is not when you are smoking two or more at the same time. When that happens, you begin to wonder why you were smoking the first one. I once burnt the back of my hand trying to put a cigarette in my mouth when there was already one there. Actually, it is not quite as stupid as it may seem. As I have already said, eventually the cigarette ceases to relieve the withdrawal pangs, and even when you are smoking the cigarette there is still something missing. This is the terrible frustration of the chain-smoker. Whenever you need the boost, you are already smoking, and this is why heavy smokers often turn to drink or other drugs. But I digress.

A combination cigarette is one occasioned by two or more of our usual reasons for smoking, such as social functions, parties, weddings, or meals in restaurants. These are examples of occasions that are both stressful and relaxing. This might at first appear to be a contradiction, but it isn't. Any form of socializing can be stressful, even with friends, and at the same time you want to be enjoying yourself and be completely relaxed.

There are situations where all four reasons for smoking are present at one and the same time. Driving can be one of these. If you are leaving a tense situation, like a visit to the dentist or the doctor, you can now relax. At the same time, driving always involves an element of stress. Your life is at stake. You are also having to concentrate. You may not be aware of the latter two factors, but the fact that they are subconscious doesn't mean they aren't there. And if you are stuck in a traffic jam or have a long highway drive, you may also be bored.

Another classic example is a game of cards. If it's a game like bridge or poker, you have to concentrate. If you are losing more than you can afford, it is stressful. If you have long periods of not getting a decent hand, it can be boring. And while all this is going on, you are at leisure—you are supposed to be relaxing. During a game of cards, no matter how slight the withdrawal pangs are, all smokers will be chain-smoking, even otherwise casual smokers. The ashtrays will fill and overflow in no time. There'll be a constant fallout cloud above head height. If you were to tap any of the smokers on the shoulder and ask him if he was enjoying it, the answer would be "You have got to be joking." It is often after nights like these, when we wake up with a throat like a cesspit, that we decide to stop smoking.

These combination cigarettes are often special ones, the ones that we think we'll miss most when we are contemplating stopping smoking. We think that life will never be quite as enjoyable again. In fact, it is the same principle at work: these cigarettes simply provide relief from withdrawal pangs, and at certain times we have greater need to relieve pangs than at others.

Let us make this quite clear. It is not the cigarette that is special; it is the occasion. Once we have removed the need for the cigarette, such occasions will become more enjoyable and the stressful situations less stressful. This will be explained in greater detail in the next chapter.

CHAPTER 14

What Am I Giving Up?

-◄O►-

ABSOLUTELY NOTHING! The thing that makes it difficult for us to give up is fear. The fear that we are being
deprived of our pleasure or prop. The fear that certain pleasant
situations will never be quite the same again. The fear of being
unable to cope with stressful situations.

In other words, the effect of brainwashing is to delude us into
believing that there is a weakness in us, or something inherent in
the cigarette that we need, and that when we stop smoking there
will be a void.

Get it clear in your mind: CIGARETTES DO NOT FILL A
VOID. THEY CREATE IT!

These bodies of ours are the most sophisticated objects on
this planet. Whether you believe in a creator, a process of natural
selection, or a combination of both, whatever being or system
devised these bodies of ours, it is immeasurably more effective
than man! Man cannot create the smallest living cell, let alone
the miracle of eyesight, reproduction, circulation, or our brains.
If the creator or process had intended us to smoke, we would

have been provided with some device to filter the poisons out of our bodies.

Our bodies are, in fact, provided with fail-safe warning devices such as coughing, dizziness, or sickness, yet we ignore these at our peril.

The beautiful truth is—there is nothing to give up. Once you purge that little monster from your body and the brainwashing from your mind, you will neither want cigarettes nor need them.

Cigarettes do not improve meals, they ruin them. They destroy our sense of taste and smell. Observe smokers in a restaurant, smoking between courses. They cannot wait for the meal to be over, as it is interfering with the cigarettes. Many smokers do it in spite of the fact that they know it offends non-smokers. It is not that smokers are generally inconsiderate people; it is just that they are miserable without the cigarette. They are between the devil and the deep blue sea. They either have to abstain and be miserable because they cannot smoke, or smoke and be miserable because they are offending other people, and feel guilty and despise themselves for it.

Watch smokers at an official function where they have to wait for the loyal toast. Many of them develop weak bladders and have to sneak off for a quick smoke. That is when you see smoking for the true addiction that it is. Smokers do not smoke because they enjoy it. They do it because they are miserable without it.

Because many of us start smoking on social occasions when we are young and shy, we acquire the belief that we cannot enjoy social occasions without a cigarette. This is nonsense. Tobacco takes away your confidence. Major evidence of the fear that cigarettes instill in smokers can be seen by their effect on women who are fastidious about their personal appearance. They wouldn't dream of appearing at a social function not immaculately turned out and smelling beautiful. Yet knowing that their breath smells like a stale ashtray does not seem to deter them in the least. I know that it *bothers* them greatly—many hate the smell of their own hair and clothes—yet it doesn't *deter* them. Such is the fear that this awful drug instills in the smoker.

Cigarettes do not help social occasions; they destroy them. Having to hold a drink in one hand and a cigarette in the other, trying to dispose of the ash and the continual chain of cigarette butts, trying not to breathe smoke and fumes into the face of the person you are conversing with, and wondering whether anyone can smell your breath or see the stains on your teeth all take away from your ability to enjoy yourself in a social situation.

Not only is there nothing to give up, but there are marvelous positive gains. When smokers contemplate quitting smoking they tend to concentrate on health, money, and social stigma. These are obviously valid and important issues, but I personally believe the greatest gains from stopping are psychological, and for varying reasons they include:

1. The return of your confidence and courage.
2. Freedom from the slavery.
3. Not having to go through life suffering the awful black shadows at the back of your mind, knowing you are being despised by half of the population, and worst of all, despising yourself.

Not only is life better as a non-smoker, it is infinitely more enjoyable. I do not just mean you will be healthier and wealthier. I mean you will be happier and enjoy life far more.

The tremendous gains from being a non-smoker are discussed in the next few chapters.

If you find it difficult to appreciate the concept of the "void," the following analogy may help.

Imagine having a cold sore on your face. I've got this marvelous ointment. I say to you, "Try this stuff." You rub the ointment on, and the sore disappears immediately. A week later it reappears. You ask, "Do you have any more of that ointment?" I say, "Keep the tube. You might need it again." You apply the ointment. Presto, the sore disappears again. Every time the sore returns, it gets larger and more painful and the interval gets shorter and shorter. Eventually the sore covers your whole face and is excruciatingly painful. It is now returning every half hour. You know that the ointment will remove it temporarily, but you are very worried. Will the sore eventually spread over your whole body? Will the interval disappear completely? You go to your doctor. He can't cure it. You try other things, but nothing helps except this marvelous ointment.

By now you are completely dependent on the ointment. You never go out without ensuring that you have a tube of the ointment with you. If you go abroad, you make sure that you take several tubes with you. Now, not only do you have worries about your health, but I'm charging you $100 per tube. You have no choice but to pay.

You then read in the medical column of your newspaper that this isn't happening just to you; many other people have been suffering from the same problem. In fact, pharmacists have discovered that the ointment doesn't actually cure the sore. All it does is reduce the sore beneath the surface of the skin. It is the ointment that has caused the sore to grow. To get rid of the sore all you have to do is stop using the ointment. The sore will eventually disappear in due course.

Would you continue to use the ointment?

Would it take willpower not to use the ointment? If you didn't believe the article, you might be apprehensive for a few days, but once you realized that the sore was beginning to get better, the need or desire to use the ointment would go.

Would you be miserable? Of course not. You had an awful problem that you thought was insoluble. Now you've found the solution. Even if it took a year for that sore to disappear completely, each day, as it improved, you'd think, "Isn't it marvelous? I'm not going to die."

This was the magic that happened to me when I extinguished that final cigarette. Let me make one point quite clear in the analogy of the sore and the ointment. The sore isn't lung cancer, or arterial sclerosis, or emphysema, or angina, or chronic asthma, or bronchitis, or coronary heart disease. They are all in addition to the sore. It isn't the thousands in cash that we burn, or the lifetime of bad breath and stained teeth, the lethargy, the wheezing and coughing, the years we spend choking ourselves and wishing we didn't, the times when we are being punished because we are not allowed to smoke. It isn't the lifetime of being despised by other people or, worst of all, despising yourself. These are all in addition to the sore. The sore is what makes us close our minds to all these things. It's that panic feeling of "I want a cigarette." Non-smokers don't suffer from that feeling. The worst thing we ever suffer from is fear, and the greatest gain you will receive is to be rid of that fear.

It was as if a great mist had suddenly lifted from my mind. I could see so clearly that that panic feeling of wanting a cigarette wasn't some sort of weakness in me, or some magic quality in the cigarette. It was caused by the first cigarette; each subsequent one, far from relieving the feeling, was causing it. At the same time I could see that all these other "happy" smokers were going through the same nightmare that I was. Not as bad as mine, but all putting up phony arguments to try to justify their stupidity.

IT'S SO NICE TO BE FREE!

CHAPTER 15

Self-Imposed Slavery

—◀O▶—

U sually when smokers try to stop, the main reasons are health, money, and social stigma. Part of the brainwashing of this awful drug is the sheer slavery.

Man fought hard in the nineteenth century to abolish slavery, and yet the smoker spends his life suffering self-imposed slavery. He seems oblivious to the fact that, when he is allowed to smoke, he wishes that he were a non-smoker. With most of the cigarettes we smoke in our lives, not only do we not enjoy them, but we aren't even aware that we are smoking them. It is only after a period of abstinence that we actually suffer the delusion of enjoying a cigarette (such as the first in the morning or the one after a meal).

The only time that the cigarette becomes precious is when we are trying to cut down or abstain, or when society forbids it (in churches, hospitals, supermarkets, theaters, and so on).

The confirmed smoker should bear in mind that this trend will get worse and worse. Soon all public places will be smoke free.

Gone are the days when the smoker could enter a friend's or stranger's house and say, "Do you mind if I smoke?" Nowadays the poor smoker, on entering a strange house, will search desperately for an ashtray and hope to find butts in it. If there is no ashtray, he will generally try to hold out, and if he cannot, he will ask for permission to smoke and is likely to be told: "Smoke if you must," or "Well, we would rather you didn't. The smell seems to linger."

The poor smoker, who was already feeling wretched, wants the ground to open up and swallow him.

I remember that during my smoking days, every time I went to church was an ordeal. Even during my own daughter's wedding, when I should have been standing there a proud father, what was I doing? I was thinking, "Let's get on with it so that we can get outside and have a drag."

> ❖
>
> **"I had previously thought I would not be able to handle stress without smoking. Now I know that I will be able to handle it better ... "**
>
> —JENNIFER O.
>
> ❖

It will help you to observe smokers on these occasions. They huddle together. There is never just one pack of cigarettes. There are twenty packs being thrust about, and the conversation is always the same.

"Do you smoke?"

"Yes, but have one of mine."

"I will have one of yours later."

They light up and take a deep drag, thinking, "Aren't we lucky? We have got our little reward. The poor non-smoker hasn't got a reward."

The "poor" non-smoker doesn't need a reward. We were not designed to go through life systematically poisoning our own bodies. The pathetic thing is that even when smoking a cigarette, the smoker doesn't achieve the feeling of peace, confidence, and tranquility that the non-smoker has experienced for the whole of his non-smoking life. The non-smoker isn't sitting in the church feeling agitated and wishing his life away. He can enjoy the whole of his life.

I can also remember playing indoor bowls in the winter and pretending to have a weak bladder in order to nip off for a puff. No, this wasn't a fourteen-year-old schoolboy, but a forty-year-old accountant. How pathetic. And even when I was back playing the game I wasn't enjoying it. I was looking forward to the finish so that I could smoke again, yet this was supposed to be my way of relaxing and enjoying my favorite hobby.

To me one of the tremendous joys of being a non-smoker is to be freed from that slavery, to be able to enjoy the whole of my life and not spend half of it craving a cigarette and then, when I light up, wishing I didn't have to do it.

Smokers should bear in mind that when they are in the houses of non-smokers or even in the company of non-smokers, it is not the self-righteous non-smoker who is depriving them, but the "little monster."

CHAPTER 16

I'll Save x Dollars a Week

◄○►

I cannot repeat too often that it is brainwashing that makes it difficult to stop smoking, and the more brainwashing we can dispel before we start, the easier it is to achieve our goal.

Occasionally I get into arguments with people whom I call confirmed smokers. By my definition a confirmed smoker is somebody who can afford it, doesn't believe it injures his health, and isn't worried about the social stigma. (There are not many about nowadays.)

If he is a young man, I say to him, "I cannot believe you are not worried about the money you are spending."

Usually his eyes light up. If I had attacked him on health grounds or on the social stigma, he would feel at a disadvantage, but on money—"Oh, I can afford it. It is only x dollars per week and I think it is worth it. It is my only vice or pleasure."

If he is a twenty-per-day smoker I say to him, "I still cannot believe you are not worried about the money. You are going to spend $100,000 or more in your lifetime. What are you doing with that money? You are not even setting light to it or throwing it away. You are actually using that money to ruin your physical health, to destroy your nerves and confidence, to suffer a lifetime of slavery, a lifetime of bad breath and stained teeth. Surely that must worry you?"

It is apparent at this point, particularly with young smokers, that they have never considered smoking a lifetime expense. For most smokers the price of a pack is bad enough. Occasionally we figure out what we spend in a week, and that is alarming. Very occasionally (and only when we think about stopping) we estimate what we spend in a year and that is frightening, but over a lifetime—it is unthinkable.

However, because it is an argument, the confirmed smoker will say, "I can afford it. It is only so much a week." He does an "encyclopedia salesman" on himself.

I then say, "I will make you an offer you cannot refuse. You pay me $2,500 now, and I will provide you with free cigarettes for the rest of your life."

If I were offering to take over a $100,000 mortgage for $2,500 the smoker would have my signature on a piece of paper before I could move, and yet not one confirmed smoker (and please bear in mind I am not now talking to someone like yourself who plans to stop, I am talking to someone who has no intention of stopping) has ever taken me up on that offer. Why not?

Often at this point in my consultation, a smoker will say, "Look, I am not really worried about the money aspect." If you are thinking along these lines, ask yourself why you are not worried. Why in other aspects of life will you go to a great deal of trouble to save a few dollars here and there and yet spend thousands of dollars poisoning yourself and hang the expense?

The answer to these questions is this. Every other decision that you make in your life is usually the result of an analytical process of weighing the pros and cons and arriving at a rational answer. It may be the wrong answer, but at least it will be the result of rational deduction. Whenever any smoker weighs the pros and cons of smoking, the answer is a dozen times over: "STOP SMOKING! YOU ARE A FOOL!" Therefore all smokers are smoking not because they want to or because they decided to, but because they think they cannot stop. They have brainwashed themselves. They have kept their heads in the sand.

The strange thing is smokers will arrange pacts among themselves, such as "First one to give in pays the other fifty dollars," yet the thousands of dollars that they would save by stopping don't seem to affect them. This is because they are still thinking with the brainwashed mind of the smoker.

Just take the sand out of your eyes for a moment. Smoking is a chain reaction and a chain for life. If you do not break that chain, you will remain a smoker for the rest of your life. Now estimate how much you think you will spend on smoking for the rest of your life. The amount will obviously vary with each individual, but for the purpose of this exercise let us assume it is $15,000.

> ❖
>
> "I feel like you've given me the wings to feel the world in its whole beauty, to have strength in my body as a 23-year-old should."
> —ZORAN K.
>
> ❖

You will shortly be making the decision to smoke your final cigarette (not yet, please—remember the initial instructions). All you have to do to remain a non-smoker is to not fall for the trap again. That is, do not smoke that first cigarette. If you do, that one cigarette will cost you $15,000 . . . .

If you think this is a tricky way of looking at it, you are still kidding yourself. Just work out how much money you would have saved if you hadn't smoked your first cigarette.

If you see the argument as factual, ask yourself how you would feel if there were a check from Publisher's Clearinghouse for $15,000 on your carpet tomorrow. You'd be dancing with delight! So start dancing! You are about to start receiving that bonus, and that's just one of the several marvelous gains you are about to receive.

During the withdrawal period you may be tempted to have just one final cigarette. It will help you resist the temptation if you remind yourself it will cost you $15,000 (or whatever your estimate is)!

I've been making that offer on television and radio for years. I still find it incredible that not one confirmed smoker has ever taken up my offer. There are members of my golf club whom I taunt every time they complain about an increase in tobacco prices. Yet, I'm frightened that if I goad them too much, one of them will take me up on it. I'd lose a fortune if he did.

If you are in the company of happy, cheerful smokers who tell you how much they enjoy it, just tell them that you know an idiot who, if paid a year's smoking money in advance, will provide them free cigarettes for the rest of their lives. Perhaps you can find me someone who will take up the offer?

CHAPTER 17

Health

—◀○▶—

This is the area where the brainwashing is the greatest. Smokers think they are aware of the health risks. They are not.

Even in my case, when I was expecting my head to explode any moment and honestly believed I was prepared to accept the consequences, I was still kidding myself. If in those days I had taken a cigarette out of the pack and a red beeper had started to sound, followed by a voice saying, "OK, Allen, this is the one! You do get a warning, and this is it. Until now you've gotten away with it, but if you smoke another cigarette your head will explode," do you think I would have lit that cigarette?

If you are in doubt about the answer, just try walking up to a main road with busy traffic, standing on the curb with your eyes closed, and trying to imagine you have the choice of either stopping smoking or walking blindfolded across the road before taking your next cigarette.

There is little doubt what your choice would be. I had been doing what every smoker does all his smoking life: closing my mind and keeping my head in the sand, hoping that I would wake up one morning and just not want to smoke anymore. Smokers cannot allow themselves to think of the health risks. If they do, even the illusion of enjoying the "habit" goes.

This explains why the shock treatment used by the media on National Smoke-Out Days is so ineffective. It is only non-smokers who can bring themselves to watch. It also explains why smokers, recalling Uncle Fred who smoked forty a day and lived until he was eighty, will ignore the thousands of people who are brought down in their prime because of this poisonous weed.

About six times a week I have the following conversation with smokers (usually the younger ones):

ME: *Why do you want to stop?*

SMOKER: *I can't afford it.*

ME: *Aren't you worried about the health risks?*

SMOKER: *No. I could step under a bus tomorrow.*

ME: *Would you deliberately step under a bus?*

SMOKER: *Of course not.*

ME: *Do you not bother to look left and right before you cross the road?*

SMOKER: *Of course I do.*

Exactly. The smoker goes to a lot of trouble not to step under a bus, and the odds are hundreds of thousands to one against it happening. Yet the smoker risks the near certainty of being crippled by the weed and appears to be completely oblivious to the risks. Such is the power of the brainwashing.

I remember one famous British golfer who wouldn't go on the American circuit because he was afraid of flying. Yet he would chain-smoke around the golf course. Isn't it strange that, if we felt there was the slightest fault in an airplane, we wouldn't go up in it even though the risks are hundreds of thousands to one against death, yet we take a one-in-four certainty with the cigarette and are apparently oblivious to the risks. And what does the smoker get out of it?

ABSOLUTELY NOTHING!

Another common myth about smoking is the smoker's cough. Many of the younger people who come to see me are not worried about their health because they do not cough. The facts are just the reverse. A cough is one of nature's fail-safe methods of dispelling foreign matter from the lungs. The cough itself is not a disease; it is just a symptom. When smokers cough it is because their lungs are trying to dispel cancer-triggering tars and poisons. When they do not cough, those tars and poisons remain in their lungs and that is when they cause cancer. Smokers tend to avoid exercise and get into the habit of shallow breathing in order not to cough. I used to believe that my permanent smoker's cough would kill me. By expelling much of the filth from my lungs, it possibly saved my life.

Just think of it this way. If you had a nice car and allowed it to rust without doing anything about it, that would be pretty stupid, as it would soon be a heap of rust and would not carry you about. However, that would not be the end of the world; it is only a question of money and you could always buy a new car. Your body is the vehicle that carries you through life. We all say that our health is our most valued asset. How true that is, as sick millionaires will tell you. Most of us can look back at some illness or accident in our lives when we prayed to get better. (HOW SOON WE FORGET.) By being a smoker you are not only letting rust get in and doing nothing about it; you are systematically destroying the vehicle you need to get through life, and you only get one.

Wise up. You don't have to do it, and remember: it is doing ABSOLUTELY NOTHING FOR YOU.

Just for a moment take your head out of the sand. Ask yourself whether, if you knew for certain that the next cigarette would be the one to trigger off cancer in your body, you would actually smoke it. Forget the disease (it is difficult to imagine it), but imagine you have to go to the hospital to suffer those awful tests—

radiation treatment and so forth. Now you are not planning the rest of your life. You are planning your death. What is going to happen to your family and loved ones, your plans and dreams?

I often see the people whom it happens to. They didn't think it would happen to them, and the worst thing about it isn't the disease itself, but the knowledge that they have brought it on themselves. All our lives as smokers we are saying, "I'll stop tomorrow." Try to imagine how those people feel who "hit the button." For them the brainwashing has ended. They then see the "habit" as it really is and spend the remainder of their lives thinking, "Why did I kid myself that I needed to smoke? If only I had the chance to go back!"

Stop kidding yourself. You have the chance. It's a chain reaction. If you smoke the next cigarette, it will lead to the next one and the next. It's already happening to you.

At the beginning of the book I promised you no shock treatment. If you have already decided to stop smoking, this won't be shock treatment for you. If you are still in doubt about stopping, skip the remainder of this chapter and come back to it when you have read the rest of the book.

Volumes of statistics have already been written about the damage that cigarettes can cause to the smoker's health. The trouble is that until the smoker decides to stop he doesn't want to know. Even the government health warning is a waste of time because the smoker puts blinders on, and if he inadvertently reads it, the first thing he does is light up a cigarette.

Smokers tend to think of the health hazard as a hit-and-miss affair, like stepping on a mine. Get it into your head: it is already happening. Every time you puff on a cigarette you are breathing cancer-triggering tars into your lungs, and cancer is by no means the worst of the killer diseases that cigarettes cause or contribute to. They are also a powerful contributing cause of heart disease, arteriosclerosis, emphysema, angina, thrombosis, chronic bronchitis, and asthma.

While I was still smoking, I'd never heard of arteriosclerosis or emphysema. I knew the permanent wheezing and coughing and the ever-increasing asthma and bronchitis attacks were a direct result of my smoking. Although they caused me discomfort there was no real pain and I could handle the discomfort.

I confess that the thought of contracting lung cancer terrified me, which is probably why I just blocked it from my mind. It's amazing how the fear of the horrendous health risks attached to smoking is overshadowed by the fear of stopping. It's not so much that the latter fear is greater, but that if we quit today the fear is immediate, whereas the fear of contracting lung cancer is a fear of the future. Why look on the black side? Perhaps it won't happen. I'm bound to have quit by then anyway.

We tend to think of smoking as a tug-of-war. On one side fear: it's unhealthy, expensive, filthy, and enslaving. On the other side the pluses: it's my pleasure, my friend, my crutch. It never seems to occur to us that this side is also fear. It's not so much that we enjoy cigarettes, but that we tend to be miserable without them.

Think of heroin addicts deprived of their heroin, the abject misery they go through. Now picture their utter joy when they are allowed to plunge a needle into their veins and end that terrible craving. Try to imagine how anyone could actually believe they get pleasure from sticking a hypodermic syringe into a vein.

Non-heroin addicts don't suffer that panic feeling. Heroin doesn't relieve the feeling, it causes it. Non-smokers don't feel miserable if they are not allowed to smoke after a meal. It's only smokers that suffer that feeling. Nicotine doesn't relieve it, it causes it.

The fear of contracting lung cancer didn't make me quit because I believed the risk was rather like walking through a minefield. If you got away with it—fine. If you were unlucky you stepped on a mine. You knew the risks you were taking and if you were prepared to take the risk, what had it to do with anyone else?

So if a non-smoker ever tried to make me aware of those risks, I would use the typical evasive tactics that all addicts invariably adopt.

"You have to die of something."
Of course you do, but is that a logical reason for deliberately shortening your life?

"Quality of life is more important than longevity."
Exactly, but you are surely not suggesting that the quality of life of an alcoholic or a heroin addict is greater than that of someone who isn't addicted to alcohol or heroin? Do you really believe that the quality of a smoker's life is better than a non-smoker's? Surely the smoker loses on both counts—his life is both shorter and more miserable.

"My lungs probably suffer more damage from car exhaust than from smoking."
Even if that were true, is that a logical reason for punishing your lungs further? Can you possibly conceive of anyone being stupid enough to actually put his or her mouth over an exhaust pipe and deliberately inhale those fumes into his or her lungs?

THAT'S WHAT SMOKERS EFFECTIVELY DO!

Think of that the next time you watch a poor smoker inhale deeply on one of those "precious" cigarettes!

I can understand why the congestion and the risks of contracting lung cancer didn't help me quit. I could cope with the former and block my mind to the latter. As you are already aware, my method is not to frighten you into quitting, but the complete opposite—to make you realize just how more enjoyable your life will be when you have escaped.

However, I do believe that if I could have seen what was happening inside my body, it would have helped me quit. I'm not referring to the shock technique of showing a smoker the color of a smoker's lungs. It was obvious to me from my nicotine-stained teeth and fingers that my lungs weren't a pretty sight. Provided they kept functioning, they were less embarrassing than my teeth and fingers—at least nobody could see my lungs.

What I am referring to is the progressive gunking-up of our arteries and veins and the gradual starving of every muscle and organ of oxygen and nutrients to be replaced with poisons and carbon monoxide (not just from car exhausts, but also from smoking).

Like the majority of motorists, I don't like the thought of dirty oil or a dirty filter in my car engine. Could you imagine buying a brand-new Rolls Royce and never changing the oil or the oil filter? That's what we effectively do to our bodies when we become smokers.

Many doctors are now relating all sorts of diseases to smoking, including diabetes, cervical cancer, and breast cancer. This is no surprise to me. The tobacco industry has belabored the fact that the medical profession has never scientifically proven that smoking is the direct cause of lung cancer.

The statistical evidence is so overwhelming as not to need proof. No one ever scientifically proved to me exactly why, when I bang my thumb with a hammer, it hurts. I soon got the message.

I must emphasize that I am not a doctor, but just as with the hammer and the thumb, it soon became obvious to me that my congestion, my permanent cough, my frequent asthma, and bronchial attacks were directly related to my smoking. However, I truly believe that the greatest hazard that smoking poses to our health is the gradual and progressive deterioration of our immune system caused by this gunking-up process.

All plants and animals on this planet are subjected to a lifetime of attack from germs, viruses, parasites, and the like. The most powerful defense we have against disease is our immune system. We all suffer infections and diseases throughout our lives. However, I do not believe that the human body was designed to be diseased, and if you are strong and healthy, your immune system will fight and defeat these attacks. How can your immune system work effectively when you are starving your muscles and organs of oxygen and nutrients and feeding them with carbon monoxide and poisons? It's not so much that smoking causes these other diseases; rather, it works like AIDS, gradually destroying your immune system.

Several of the adverse effects that smoking had on my health, some of which I had been suffering from for years, did not become apparent to me until many years after I had stopped smoking.

While I was busy despising those idiots and cranks who would rather lose their legs than quit smoking, it didn't even occur to me that I was already suffering from arteriosclerosis myself. I attributed my almost permanently gray complexion to my natural coloring or to lack of exercise. It never occurred to me that it was really due to the blocking up of my capillaries. I had varicose veins in my thirties, which have miraculously disappeared since I stopped smoking. About five years before I stopped I reached the stage when every night I would have this weird sensation in my legs. It wasn't a sharp pain or like pins and needles, just a sort of restless feeling. I would get my wife, Joyce, to massage my legs every night. It didn't occur to me until at least a year after I had stopped that I no longer needed the massage.

About two years before I quit, I would occasionally get violent pains in my chest, which I feared must be lung cancer, but now assume to have been angina. I haven't had a single attack since I quit.

When I was a child I would bleed profusely from cuts. This frightened me. No one explained to me that bleeding was in fact a natural and essential healing process and that the blood would clot when its healing purpose was completed. I suspected that I was a hemophiliac and feared that I might bleed to death. Later in life I would sustain quite deep cuts yet hardly bleed at all. This brown-red gunk would ooze from the cut.

The color worried me. I knew that blood was meant to be bright red and I assumed that I had some sort of blood disease.

However, I was pleased about the consistency, which meant that I no longer bled profusely. Not until after I had stopped smoking did I learn that smoking coagulated the blood and that the brownish color was due to lack of oxygen. I was ignorant of the effect at the time, but in hindsight, it was this effect that smoking was having on my health that most fills me with horror. When I think of my poor heart trying to pump that gunk around restricted blood vessels, day in and day out, without missing a single beat, I find it a miracle that I didn't suffer a stroke or a heart attack. It made me realize not how fragile our bodies are, but what strong and ingenious machines they are!

I had liver spots on my hands in my forties—those brown or white spots that very old people have on their face and hands. I tried to ignore them, assuming that they were due to early senility caused by the hectic lifestyle that I led. It was five years after I had quit that a smoker at the Raynes Park clinic remarked that when he had stopped previously, his liver spots had disappeared. I had forgotten about mine, and to my amazement, they too had disappeared.

As long as I can remember, I had spots flashing in front of my eyes if ever I stood up too quickly, particularly if I was in a bath. I would feel dizzy, as if I were about to black out. I never related this to smoking. In fact, I was convinced that it was quite normal and that everyone else had a similar reaction. Not until ten years ago, when an ex-smoker told me that he no longer had that sensation, did it occur to me that I no longer had it either.

One of the great evils about smoking is that it fools us into believing that nicotine gives us courage, when in fact it gradually and imperceptibly dissipates it. I was shocked when I heard my father say that he had no wish to live to be fifty. Little did I realize that twenty years later I would have exactly the same lack of joie de vivre. You might conclude that this chapter has been one of necessary, or unnecessary, doom and gloom. I promise you it is the complete opposite. I used to fear death when I was a child. I used to believe that smoking removed that fear. Perhaps it did. If so, it replaced it with something infinitely worse: A FEAR OF LIVING!

Now my fear of dying has returned. It does not bother me. I realize that it only exists because I now enjoy life so much. I don't brood over my fear of dying any more than I did when I was a child. I'm far too busy living my life to the fullest. The odds are against my living to a hundred, but I'll try to. I'll also try to enjoy every precious moment!

There were two other advantages on the health side that never occurred to me until I had stopped smoking. One was that I used to have repetitive nightmares every night. I would dream that I was being chased. I can only assume that these nightmares were the result of my body being deprived of nicotine throughout the night and the insecure feeling that caused. Now the only nightmare that I have is that I occasionally dream that I am smoking again. This is quite a common dream among ex-smokers. Some worry that it means that they are still subconsciously pining for a cigarette. Don't worry about it. The fact that it was a nightmare means that you are very pleased not to be a smoker. There is that twilight zone after any nightmare when you wake up and are not sure whether it is a genuine catastrophe, but isn't it marvelous when you realize that it was only a dream?

When I described being chased every night in a dream, I originally typed "chaste." Perhaps this was just a Freudian slip, but it does give me a convenient lead into the second advantage. At clinics, when covering the effect that smoking has on concentration, I would sometimes say: "Which organ in your body has the greatest need of a good supply of blood?" The stupid grins, usually on the faces of the men, would indicate that they had missed the point. However, they were absolutely right. Being a somewhat shy Englishman, I find the subject rather embarrassing, and I have no intention of doing a miniature Kinsey report by going into detail about the adverse effect that smoking had on my own sexual activity and enjoyment, or that of other ex-smokers with whom I have discussed the subject. Again, I was not aware of this effect until sometime after I had stopped smoking and had attributed my sexual prowess and activity, or rather lack of it, to advancing years.

However, if you watch nature films, you will be aware that the first rule of nature is survival, and that the second rule is survival of the species, or reproduction. Nature ensures that reproduction does not take place unless the partners feel physically healthy and know that they have secured a safe home, territory, supply of food, and a suitable mate. Man's ingenuity has enabled him to bend these rules somewhat; however, I know for a fact that smoking can lead to impotency. I can also assure you that when you feel fit and healthy, you'll enjoy sex much more, and more often.

❖

"All the life situations that terrified me before and that I thought I would not be able to deal with without a cigarette are no problem. So I just want to say thank you."
—PETI D.

❖

Smokers also suffer the illusion that the ill effects of smoking are overstated. The reverse is the case. There is no doubt that cigarettes are the number one cause of preventable death in society. The trouble is that in many cases where cigarettes cause the death or are a contributing factor, it is not blamed on cigarettes in the statistics.

It has been estimated that forty-four percent of household fires are caused by cigarettes. I wonder how many road accidents have been caused by cigarettes during that split second the driver takes his eye off the road to light up.

I am normally a careful driver, but the nearest I came to death (except from smoking itself) was when trying to roll a cigarette while driving. I hate to think of the number of times I coughed a cigarette out of my mouth while driving—it always seemed to end up between the seats. I am sure many other smoking drivers have had the experience of trying to locate the burning cigarette with one hand while trying to drive with the other.

The effect of the brainwashing is that we tend to think like the man who, having fallen from a hundred-story building, is heard to say as he passes the fiftieth floor, "So far, so good!" We think that since we've gotten away with it so far, one more cigarette won't make the difference.

Try to see it another way: the "habit" is a continuous chain for life, each cigarette creating the need for the next. When you start the habit you light a fuse. The trouble is, YOU DON'T KNOW HOW LONG THE FUSE IS. Every time you light a cigarette you are one step nearer to the bomb exploding. HOW WILL YOU KNOW IF IT'S THE NEXT ONE?

CHAPTER 18

Energy

—◁ ○ ▷—

Most smokers are aware of the effect that this progressive process of gunking-up and starvation of oxygen and nutrients has on their lungs. However, they are not so aware of the effect it has on their energy level.

One of the subtleties of the smoking trap is that the effects it has on us, both physical and mental, happen so gradually and imperceptibly that we are not aware of them and regard them as normal.

It is very similar to the effects of bad eating habits. The potbelly appears so gradually that it causes us no alarm. We look at people who are grossly overweight and wonder how they could possibly have allowed themselves to reach that state.

But supposing it happened overnight. You went to bed weighing 140 pounds, trim, rippling with muscles, and not an ounce of fat on your body. You awoke weighing 182 pounds, fat, bloated and potbellied. Instead of waking up feeling fully rested and full of energy, you wake up feeling miserable, lethargic, and you can hardly open your eyes. You would be panic-stricken, wondering what awful disease you had contracted overnight. Yet the disease is exactly the same. The fact that it took twenty years to reach that state is irrelevant.

So it is with smoking. If I could immediately transfer you into the mind and body you would have after having stopped smoking for just three weeks, that is all I would need to do to persuade you to quit. You would think: "Will I really feel this good?" Or what it really amounts to: "Have I really sunk that low?" I emphasize that I don't just mean how much healthier and energetic you would feel, but also how much more confident, relaxed, and mentally sharp you would feel.

As a teenager, I can remember rushing around just for the hell of it. Then, for thirty-odd years, I became permanently tired and lethargic. I used to struggle to wake up at nine o'clock in the morning. After dinner I would lie on a couch watching television and nod off after five minutes. Because my father used to be the same, I thought this behavior was normal. I believed that energy was the exclusive prerogative of children and teenagers, and that old age began in the early twenties.

❖

"I never thought that I could make it through a day without smoking. Now. . . . I can't believe I ever smoked for so long and lived in so much fear of going without."

—BEVERLY J.

❖

Shortly after I extinguished my final cigarette, I was relieved that the congestion and the coughing disappeared, and I haven't had an asthma or bronchitis attack since. However, something truly marvelous and unexpected also happened. I started waking at seven o'clock in the morning feeling completely rested and full of energy, actually wanting to exercise, jog, and swim. At forty-eight I couldn't run a step or swim a stroke. My sporting activities were confined to such dynamic pursuits as lawn bowling, affectionately referred to as the old man's game, and golf, for which I had to use a motorized cart. At the age of sixty-nine, I exercise for half an hour and swim daily. It's great to have energy, and when you feel physically and mentally strong, it feels great to be alive.

The problem is that when you quit smoking, the return of your physical and mental health is also gradual. True, it's not nearly as slow as the slide into the pit, and if you are going through the trauma of the Willpower Method of quitting, any health or financial gains will be obliterated by the depression you will likely be going through.

Unfortunately, I cannot immediately transfer you into the mind and body you could have in three weeks' time. But you can! You know instinctively that what I am telling you is correct. All you need to do is: USE YOUR IMAGINATION!

CHAPTER 19

It Relaxes Me and Gives Me Confidence

—◁○▷—

That smoking is relaxing and gives you confidence is the worst fallacy of all. For me, ending the slavery to cigarettes has been the greatest benefit from quitting. You no longer have to go through life with the permanent feeling of insecurity that smokers suffer from.

Smokers find it very difficult to believe that the cigarette actually causes that insecure feeling you get when you are out late at night and running out of cigarettes. Non-smokers do not suffer from that feeling. It is the tobacco that causes it.

I only became aware of many of the advantages of stopping months afterwards, as a result of my consultations with other smokers.

For twenty-five years I refused to have a physical. If I wanted life insurance, I insisted on "no physical" and paid higher premiums as a result. I hated visiting hospitals, doctors, or dentists. I couldn't face the thought of aging, pensions, and so on.

I related none of these things to my smoking "habit," but getting off it has been like awakening from a bad dream. Nowadays I look forward to each day. Of course, bad things happen in my life, and I am subject to the normal stresses and strains, but it is wonderful to have the confidence to cope with them. The extra health, energy, and confidence make the good times more enjoyable too.

CHAPTER 20

Those Sinister Black Shadows

—◄○►—

Another of the great joys of quitting the weed is to be free of those sinister black shadows at the back of our minds.

All smokers know they are fools and close their minds to the ill effects of smoking. For most of our lives smoking is automatic, but the black shadows are always lurking in our subconscious minds just beneath the surface.

There are several marvelous advantages to achieve from quitting smoking. Some of them I was consciously aware of throughout my smoking life, such as the health benefits, saving money, and freedom from self-imposed slavery. However, so obsessed was I in resisting all the attempts of do-gooders and anyone else who tried to persuade me to quit, that all my imagination and energy were directed to finding any flimsy excuse that would allow me to continue to smoke.

Amazingly, my most ingenious thoughts occurred when I was actually trying to quit. They were of course inspired by the fear and misery I suffered when attempting to quit by using willpower. No way could I block my mind from the health and financial aspects. But now that I am free it amazes me how I successfully blocked my mind from even more important advantages of quitting. I've already mentioned the sheer slavery—spending half our lives being allowed to smoke, doing it automatically and wishing we had never started, the other half feeling miserable and deprived because society won't allow us to smoke. In the last chapter I referred to the incredible joy of having energy again. But for me the greatest joy of being free was not the health, the money, the energy, or the ending of the slavery, it was the removal of those sinister black shadows—those feelings of being despised by and apologetic to non-smokers. With those black shadows gone, I finally regained the ability to respect myself.

Most smokers aren't the weak-willed, spineless jellyfish that society tends to believe them to be. In every other aspect of my life I was in control. I loathed myself for being dependent on an evil weed that I knew was ruining my life. I cannot tell you of the utter joy of being free from those sinister black shadows, the dependency, and the self-loathing. I can't tell you how nice it is to be able to look at all other smokers, whether they be young, old, casual, or heavy, not with a feeling of envy, but with a feeling of pity for them—and elation for you that you are no longer the slave of that insidious weed.

The last two chapters have dealt with the considerable advantages of being a non-smoker. I feel it necessary to give a balanced account, so the next chapter lists the advantages of being a smoker.

CHAPTER 21

The Advantages of Being a Smoker

◄○►

CHAPTER 22

The Willpower Method of Stopping

---◄○►---

It is an accepted fact in our society that it is very difficult to stop smoking. Even books advising you how to do so usually start off by telling you how difficult it is. The truth is that it is ridiculously easy. Yes, I can understand your questioning that statement, but just consider it.

If your aim is to run a mile in under four minutes, that's difficult. You may have to undergo years of hard training, and even then you may be physically incapable of doing it. (Much of our achievement lies in the mind. Isn't it strange how difficult a four-minute mile was until Roger Bannister actually did it, but nowadays it is commonplace?)

However, in order to stop smoking all you have to do is not smoke anymore. No one forces you to smoke (apart from yourself), and unlike food or drink, you don't need it to survive. So if you want to stop doing it, why should it be difficult? In fact, it isn't. It is smokers who make it difficult by using the Willpower

Method. I define the Willpower Method as any method that forces the smoker to feel he is making some sort of sacrifice. Let us just consider the Willpower Method.

We do not decide to become smokers. We merely experiment with the first few cigarettes and because they taste awful we are convinced that we can stop whenever we want to. In the beginning, we smoke those first few cigarettes only when we want to, and that is usually in the company of other smokers on social occasions.

Before we realize it, we are not only buying cigarettes regularly and smoking when we want to, we are smoking every day. Smoking has become a part of our lives. We ensure that we always have cigarettes on our person. We believe that social occasions and meals are improved by them and that they relieve stress. It doesn't seem to occur to us that the same cigarette out of the same pack will taste exactly the same after a meal as it does first thing in the morning. In fact, smoking neither improves meals and social occasions, nor does it relieve stress. It's just that smokers believe they can't enjoy a meal or handle stress without a cigarette.

It usually takes us a long time to realize that we are hooked because we suffer from the illusion that we smoke because we enjoy a cigarette, not because we have to have a cigarette. While we are not enjoying cigarettes (which we never do), we suffer from the illusion that we can stop whenever we want to.

Usually it is not until we actually try to stop that we realize a problem exists. The first attempts to stop are more often than not in the early days and are usually triggered by shortage of money (boy meets girl and they are saving to set up home and do not want to waste money on cigarettes) or health concerns (the teenager is still active in sports and finds he is short of breath). Whatever the reason, the smoker always waits for a stressful situation. As soon as he stops, the little monster needs feeding. The smoker then wants a cigarette, and because he cannot have one he feels more distressed. The thing he usually takes to relieve stress is now not available, so he suffers a triple blow. The probable result after a period of torture is the compromise "I'll cut down" or "I've picked the wrong time" or "I'll wait until the stress has gone from my life." However, once the stress has gone, he has no need to stop and doesn't decide to do so again until the next stressful time. Of course, the time is never right because life for most people doesn't become less stressful; it becomes more so. We leave the protection of our parents and enter the world of setting up home, taking on mortgages, having children, working responsible jobs, and so forth. Of course, the smoker's life can never become less stressful because it is the cigarette that actually causes stress. As the smoker's rate of nicotine intake rises, the more distressed he becomes and the greater the illusion of his dependency becomes.

In fact, it is an illusion that life becomes more stressful, and it's the smoking itself, or a similar crutch, that creates the illusion. This will be discussed in greater detail in chapter 28.

After the initial failures, the smoker usually relies on the possibility that one day he will wake up and just not want to smoke anymore. This hope is usually kindled by the stories that he has heard about other ex-smokers (such as, "I had a bout of flu and afterwards I didn't want to smoke anymore.")

Don't kid yourself. I have probed all of these rumors, and they are never quite as simple as they appear. Usually the smoker has already been preparing himself to stop and merely used the flu as a springboard. I spent thirty-odd years waiting to wake up one morning wanting never to smoke again. But whenever I had a bad cold I would look forward to its ending because it was interfering with my smoking.

More often in the case of people who stop "just like that" they have suffered a shock. Perhaps a close relative has died from a cigarette-related disease or they have had a scare themselves. It is so much easier to say, "I just decided to stop one day. That's the sort of guy I am." Stop kidding yourself! It won't happen unless you make it happen.

Let's consider in greater detail why the Willpower Method is so difficult. For most of our lives we adopt the head-in-the-sand "I'll stop tomorrow" approach.

At odd times something will trigger an attempt to stop. It may be concern about health, money, or social stigma, or we may have been going through a particularly heavy bout of choking and realize that we don't actually enjoy it.

Whatever the reason, we take our head out of the sand and start weighing the pros and cons of smoking. We then find out what we have known all our lives: on a rational assessment the conclusion is, a dozen times over, STOP SMOKING.

If you were to sit down and give points for all the advantages of stopping and do a similar exercise with the advantages of smoking, the total point count for stopping would far outweigh that for continuing.

However, although the smoker knows that he will be better off as a non-smoker, he believes that by quitting he is making a sacrifice. Although it is an illusion, it is a *powerful* illusion. The smoker doesn't know why, but he believes that during the good times and the bad times of life the cigarette does appear to help.

Before he starts the attempts to quit, he is affected by the brainwashing of our society, reinforced by the brainwashing of his own addiction. To these must be added the even more powerful brainwashing of "how difficult it is to give up."

He's heard stories of smokers who have stopped for many months and are still desperately craving a cigarette. He's heard of the disgruntled stoppers—those who stop and then spend the rest of their lives bemoaning the fact that they'd love a cigarette. He's heard of smokers who have stopped for many years, apparently leading happy lives, but have one cigarette and are suddenly hooked again. Probably he also knows several smokers in the advanced stages of the disease who are visibly destroying themselves and are clearly not enjoying cigarettes—yet they continue to smoke. Added to all this, he has probably already suffered one or more of these experiences himself.

So, instead of starting with the feeling, "Great! Have you heard the news? I don't have to smoke anymore," he starts with a feeling of doom and gloom, as if he were trying to climb Mount Everest. He firmly believes that once the little monster has got his hooks into you, you are hooked for life. Many smokers even start the attempt by apologizing to their friends and relatives: "Look, I am trying to give up smoking. I will probably be irritable during the next few weeks. Try to bear with me." Most attempts are doomed before they start.

Let's assume that the smoker survives a few days without a cigarette. The congestion is rapidly disappearing from his lungs. He hasn't bought cigarettes and consequently has more money in his pocket. So the reasons why he decided to stop in the first place are rapidly disappearing from his thoughts. It is like seeing a bad road accident when you are driving. It slows you down for a while, but the next time you are late for an appointment you have forgotten all about it and your foot stamps on the throttle.

On the other side of the tug-of-war, that little monster inside your stomach hasn't had his fix. There is no physical pain; if you had the same feeling because of a cold, you wouldn't stop working or get depressed. You would laugh it off. All the smoker knows is that he wants a cigarette. Why it is so important to him he doesn't know. The little monster in the stomach then triggers the big monster in the mind, and soon the person who a few hours or days earlier was listing all the reasons to stop smoking is desperately searching for any excuse to start again. Now he is saying things like:

1. Life is too short. The bomb could go off. I could get hit by a bus tomorrow. I have left it too late. Everything gives you cancer these days.

2. I have picked the wrong time. I should have waited until after the holidays/after my vacation/after this stressful event in my life.

3. I cannot concentrate. I am getting irritable and bad tempered. I cannot do my job properly. My family and friends won't love me. Let's face it, for everybody's sake I need to start smoking again. I am a confirmed smoker and there is no way I will ever be happy again without a cigarette. (This one kept me smoking for thirty-three years.)

At this stage the smoker usually gives in. He lights a cigarette and the schizophrenia increases. On the one hand there is the tremendous relief of ending the craving, when the little monster finally gets his fix; on the other hand, if the smoker has survived a long time without a cigarette, it tastes awful and the smoker cannot understand why he is smoking it. This is why the smoker thinks he lacks willpower. In fact, it is not lack of willpower. He has simply changed his mind and made a perfectly rational decision in light of the latest information. What's the point of being healthy if you are miserable? What is the point of being rich if you are miserable? There is none. It is far better to have a shorter enjoyable life than a lengthy miserable life.

Fortunately, the smoker's rationale does not reflect the truth. Life as a non-smoker is infinitely more enjoyable, yet it was the delusion that it is *less* enjoyable that kept me smoking for thirty-three years, and I must confess, if that were the true situation, I would still be smoking (correction—I wouldn't be here).

The misery that the smoker is suffering has nothing to do with withdrawal pangs. True, pangs trigger the misery, but the actual agony is in the mind, caused by doubt and uncertainty. Because the smoker starts by feeling he is making a sacrifice, he begins to feel deprived—this is a form of stress. One of the times when his brain tells him, "Have a cigarette," is a time of stress. Therefore as soon as he stops smoking, he wants a cigarette. But now he can't have one because he has stopped smoking. This makes him more depressed, which sets the trigger off again.

Another thing that makes it so difficult is that you are waiting for something to happen. If your object is to pass a driving test, as soon as you have passed the test it is certain you have achieved your object. Under the Willpower Method you say, "If I can go long enough without a cigarette, the urge to smoke will eventually go."

How do you know when you have achieved it? The answer is that you never do because you are waiting for something to happen and nothing else is going to happen. You stopped when you smoked that last cigarette, and what you are really doing now is waiting to see how long it will be before you give in.

As I said above, the agony that the smoker undergoes is mental, caused by the uncertainty. Although there is no physical pain, the mental agony still has a powerful effect. The smoker is miserable and insecure. Far from forgetting about smoking, his mind becomes obsessed with it.

There can be days or even weeks of black depression. His mind is obsessed with doubts and fears.

"How long will the craving last?"

"Will I ever be happy again?"

"Will I ever want to get up in the morning?"

"Will I ever enjoy a meal again?"

"How will I ever cope with stress in the future?"

"Will I ever enjoy a social function again?"

The smoker is waiting for things to improve, but of course while he is still moping, the cigarette is becoming more precious.

In fact, something does happen, but the smoker isn't conscious of it. If he can survive three weeks without inhaling any nicotine at all, the physical craving for nicotine disappears. However, as stated before, the pangs of withdrawal from nicotine are so mild that the smoker isn't aware of them. But after about three weeks many smokers sense that they have "kicked it." They then light a cigarette to prove it, and it does just that. It tastes awful, but the ex-smoker has now supplied nicotine to the body, and as soon as he extinguishes that cigarette the nicotine starts to leave the body. There is now a little voice at the back of his mind saying, "You want another one." In fact, he had kicked it, but now he has hooked himself again.

The smoker will not usually light another cigarette immediately. He thinks, "I don't want to get hooked again." So he allows a safe period to pass. It might be hours, days, even weeks. The ex-smoker can now say, "Well, I didn't get hooked, so I can safely have another." He has fallen into the same trap as he did in the first place and is already on the slippery slope.

Smokers who succeed under the Willpower Method tend to find it long and difficult because the main problem is the brainwashing, and long after the physical addiction has died the smoker is still moping about cigarettes. Eventually, if he can survive long enough, it begins to dawn on him that he is not going to give in. He stops moping and accepts that life goes on and is enjoyable without the cigarette.

Many smokers are succeeding with this method, but it is difficult and arduous, and there are many more failures than successes. Even those who do succeed go through the rest of their lives in a vulnerable state. They are left with a certain amount of brainwashing and still believe that the cigarette can give you a boost. (Most non-smokers also suffer from that illusion. They are subjected to brainwashing also, but either find they cannot learn to "enjoy" smoking or don't want the bad side, thank you very much.) This explains why many smokers who have stopped for long periods start smoking again.

Many ex-smokers will have the occasional cigar or cigarette either as a "special treat" or to convince themselves how awful it is. It does exactly that, but as soon as they put it out the nicotine starts to leave and a little voice at the back of their mind is saying, "You want another one." If they light another one, it still tastes awful and they say, "Marvelous! While I am not enjoying it I won't get hooked. After the holidays/vacation/ this trauma, I will stop."

Too late. They are already hooked. The trap that they fell into in the first place has claimed its victim again.

As I keep saying, enjoyment doesn't come into it. It never did! If we smoked because we enjoyed it, nobody would ever smoke more than one cigarette. We assume we enjoy cigarettes only because we cannot believe we would be stupid enough to smoke if we didn't enjoy them. This is why so much of our smoking is subconscious. If, while smoking every cigarette, you were aware of the foul fumes going into your lungs and you had to say to yourself, "This is going to cost $100,000 in my lifetime, and this cigarette might just be the one to trigger cancer in my lungs," even the illusion of enjoyment would go. When we try to block our minds to the bad side, we feel stupid. If we had to face up to it, that would be intolerable! If you watch smokers, particularly at social functions, you will see that they are happy only when they are not aware that they are smoking. Once they become aware of it, they tend to be uncomfortable and apologetic. You smoke to feed that little monster . . . and once you have purged the little monster from your body and the big monster from your brain, you will have neither need nor desire to smoke.

CHAPTER 23

Beware of Cutting Down

—◀○▶—

Many smokers resort to cutting down either as a stepping-stone towards stopping or as an attempt to control the little monster, and many doctors and advisers recommend cutting down as an aid.

Obviously, the less you smoke the better off you are, but as a stepping-stone to stopping, cutting down is fatal. It is our attempts to cut down that keep us trapped all our lives.

Cutting down usually follows failed attempts to stop. After a few hours or days of abstinence the smoker says to himself something like, "I cannot face the thought of being without a cigarette, so from now on I will just smoke the special ones or I will cut down to ten a day. If I can get in the habit of smoking ten a day, I can either hold it there or cut down further."

Certain terrible things now happen.

1. He has the worst of all worlds. He is still addicted to nicotine and is keeping the monster alive not only in his body but also in his mind.

2. He is now wishing his life away waiting for the next cigarette.

3. Prior to cutting down, whenever he wanted a cigarette, he lit one up and at least partially relieved his withdrawal pangs. Now, in addition to the normal stresses and strains of life, he is actually causing himself to suffer the withdrawal pangs from nicotine most of his life. So he is causing himself to be miserable and bad tempered.

4. While he was indulging himself, he didn't enjoy most of the cigarettes and he didn't realize he was smoking them. It was automatic. The only cigarettes that he imagined he enjoyed were after a period of abstinence (such as the first in the morning or the one after a meal).

Now that he waits an extra hour for each cigarette, he "enjoys" every one. The longer he waits, the more enjoyable each cigarette appears to become because the "enjoyment" in a cigarette isn't the cigarette itself; it's the ending of the agitation caused by the craving, whether it be the slight physical craving for nicotine or the mental moping. The longer you suffer, the more "enjoyable" each cigarette becomes.

The main difficulty of stopping smoking is not the chemical addiction. That's easy. Smokers will go all night without a cigarette; the craving doesn't even wake them up. Many smokers will actually leave the bedroom before they light up. Many will actually have breakfast. Some will even wait until they arrive at work.

They will go ten hours without a cigarette and it doesn't bother them. If they went ten hours during the day without one, they would be tearing their hair out.

Many smokers will buy a new car and abstain from smoking in it. Smokers will visit supermarkets, theaters, doctors, hospitals, and dentists without undue inconvenience. Many smokers will abstain in the company of non-smokers. Smokers are almost pleased for someone to say they cannot smoke. In fact, smokers get a secret pleasure out of going long periods without a cigarette. It gives them the hope that maybe one day they will never want another one.

The real problem when stopping smoking is the brainwashing, the illusion that the cigarette is some sort of prop or reward and life will never be quite the same without it. Far from turning you off smoking, all cutting down does is leave you feeling insecure and miserable. It convinces you that the most precious thing on this earth is the next cigarette, that there is no way that you will ever be happy again without one.

There is nothing more pathetic than the smoker who is trying to cut down. He suffers from the delusion that the less he smokes, the less he will want to smoke. In fact, the reverse is true. The less he smokes, the longer he suffers the withdrawal pangs; the more he enjoys the cigarette, the more distasteful they become. But that won't stop him from smoking. Taste never ever came into it. If smokers smoked because they enjoyed the taste, nobody would ever smoke more than one cigarette. You find that difficult to believe? OK, let's talk it out. Which is the worst tasting cigarette? That's right, the first in the morning, the one that during the winter sets us coughing and spluttering. Which is one of the most precious cigarettes for most smokers? That's right, the first cigarette in the morning! Now, do you really believe you are smoking it to enjoy the taste and smell, or do you think a more rational explanation is that you are relieving nine hours' worth of withdrawal pangs?

It is essential that we remove all the illusions about smoking before extinguishing that final cigarette. Unless you've removed the illusion that you enjoy the taste of certain cigarettes before you extinguish the final one, there is no way you can prove it afterwards without getting hooked again. So, unless you are already smoking one, light one up now. Inhale six deep breaths of that glorious tobacco and ask yourself what is so glorious about the taste. Perhaps you believe that it is only certain cigarettes that taste good, like the one after a meal. If so, why do you bother to smoke the others? Because you got into the habit of doing it? Now why would anyone get into the habit of smoking cigarettes that he or she finds distasteful? And why should the same cigarette out of the same pack taste different after a meal than it tastes first thing in the morning? Food doesn't taste different after a cigarette, so why should a cigarette taste different after food?

Don't just rely on me. Check it out: smoke a cigarette consciously after a meal to prove that it tastes no different. The reason smokers believe that cigarettes taste better after a meal or at social occasions with alcohol is that those are the times when both non-smokers and smokers are really happy, but a nicotine addict can never be really happy if that little nicotine monster remains unsatisfied. It's not so much that smokers enjoy the taste of tobacco after a meal; after all, we don't eat tobacco, so where does taste come into it? It's just that smokers are miserable if they aren't allowed to relieve their withdrawal symptoms at those times. So the difference between smoking and not smoking is the difference between being happy and miserable. That's why the cigarette appears to taste better. Whereas smokers who light up first thing in the morning are miserable whether they are smoking or not.

❖

"I can now swim, cycle, surf, windsurf, and run again without being caught for breath and having to use an inhaler every thirty minutes."
—KEVIN M.

❖

Cutting down not only doesn't work, but it is also the worst form of torture. It doesn't work because initially the smoker hopes that by getting into the habit of smoking less and less, he will reduce his desire to smoke a cigarette. It is not a habit. It is an addiction, and the nature of any addiction is to want more and more, not less and less. Therefore in order to cut down, the smoker has to exercise willpower and discipline for the rest of his life.

The main problem of stopping smoking is not the chemical addiction to nicotine. That's easy to cope with. It is the mistaken belief that the cigarette gives you some pleasure. This mistaken belief is brought about initially by the brainwashing we receive before we start smoking, which is then reinforced by the actual addiction. All cutting down does is reinforce the fallacy further to the extent that smoking dominates the smoker's life completely and convinces him that the most precious thing on this earth is the next cigarette.

As I have already said, cutting down never works anyway because you have to exercise willpower and discipline for the rest of your life. If you didn't have enough willpower to stop, then you certainly don't have enough to cut down. Stopping is far easier and less painful.

I have heard of literally thousands of cases in which cutting down has failed. The handful of successes I have known have been achieved after a relatively short period of cutting down, followed by going "cold turkey." The smokers really stopped in spite of cutting down, not because of it. All it did was prolong the agony. A failed attempt to cut down leaves the smoker a nervous wreck, even more convinced that he is hooked for life. This is usually enough to keep him puffing away for another five years before the next attempt.

However, cutting down illustrates the whole futility of smoking because it clearly shows that a cigarette is enjoyable only after a period of abstinence. You have to bang your head against a brick wall (that is, suffer withdrawal pangs) to make it nice when you stop.

So the choice is:

1. Cut down for life. This will be self-imposed torture, and you will not be able to do it anyway.

2. Increasingly choke yourself for life. What is the point?

3. Be nice to yourself. Stop doing it.

The other important point that cutting down demonstrates is that there is no such thing as the odd or occasional cigarette. Smoking is a chain reaction that will last the rest of your life unless you make a positive effort to break it.

REMEMBER: CUTTING DOWN WILL DRAG YOU DOWN.

CHAPTER 24

Just One Cigarette

—◄○►—

"Just one cigarette" is a myth you must get out of your mind. It is just one cigarette that gets us started in the first place.

It is just one cigarette to tide us over a difficult patch or on a special occasion that defeats most of our attempts to stop.

It is just one cigarette that, when smokers have succeeded in breaking the addiction, sends them back into the trap. Sometimes it is just to confirm that they do not need them anymore, and that one cigarette does just that. It tastes horrible and convinces the smoker he will never become hooked again, but he already is.

It is the thought of that one special cigarette that often prevents smokers from stopping—that first one in the morning or the one after a meal.

Get it firmly in your mind that there is no such thing as just one cigarette. It is a chain reaction that will last the rest of your life unless you break it.

It is the myth about the odd, special cigarette that keeps smokers moping about it when they stop. Get into the habit of never seeing the odd cigarette or pack—it is a fantasy. Whenever you think about smoking, see a whole filthy lifetime of spending a small fortune just for the privilege of destroying yourself mentally and physically, a lifetime of slavery, a lifetime of bad breath.

It is a pity that there isn't something like a cigarette that, during good and bad times, we can use for an occasional boost or pleasure. But get it clearly into your mind: the cigarette isn't it. You are stuck with either a lifetime of misery or none at all. You wouldn't dream of taking cyanide because you liked the taste of almonds, so stop punishing yourself with the thought of the occasional cigarette or cigar.

Ask a smoker, "If you had the opportunity to go back to the time before you became hooked, would you have become a smoker?" The answer is inevitably, "You have got to be joking," yet every smoker has that choice every day of his life. Why doesn't he opt for it? The answer is fear. The fear that he cannot stop or that life won't be the same without it.

Stop kidding yourself. You can do it. Anybody can. It's ridiculously easy.

In order to make it easy to stop smoking there are certain fundamentals to get clear in your mind. We have already dealt with three of them up to now:

1. There is nothing to give up. There are only marvelous positive gains to achieve.

2. Never visualize the odd cigarette. It doesn't exist. There is only a lifetime of filth and disease.

3. There is nothing different about you. Any smoker can find it easy to stop.

Many smokers believe that they are confirmed smokers or have addictive personalities. I promise you there is no such thing. No one needs to smoke before he or she becomes hooked on the drug. It is the drug that hooks you and not the nature of your character or personality. That is the effect of these drugs: they make you believe that you have an addictive personality. However, it is essential that you remove this belief, because if you believe that you are dependent on nicotine, you will be, even after the little nicotine monster inside your body is dead. It is essential to remove all of the brainwashing.

CHAPTER 25

Casual Smokers, Teenagers, Non-Smokers

—◀○▶—

Heavy smokers tend to envy casual smokers. We've all met these characters: "Oh, I can go all week without a cigarette, it really doesn't bother me." We think: "I wish I were like that." I know this is hard to believe, but no smoker enjoys being a smoker. Never forget:

○ No smoker ever decided to become a smoker, casual or otherwise, therefore:

○ All smokers feel stupid, therefore:

○ All smokers have to lie to themselves and other people in a vain attempt to justify their stupidity.

I used to be a golf fanatic. I would brag about how often I played and I wanted to play more. Why do smokers brag about how little they smoke? If that's the true criterion, then surely the true accolade is not to smoke at all.

If I said to you, "Do you know, I can go all week without carrots and it doesn't bother me in the slightest," you would think I was some sort of nutcase. If I enjoy carrots, why would I want go all week without them? If I don't enjoy them, why would I make such a statement? So when a smoker makes a statement like "I can go all week without a cigarette, it really doesn't bother me," he's trying to convince both himself and you that he has no problem. But there would be no need to make the statement if he had no problem. What he is really saying is: "I managed to survive a whole week without smoking." Like every smoker, he was probably hoping that after this he could survive the rest of his life. But he could only survive a week, and can you imagine how precious that cigarette must have been, having felt deprived for a whole week?

This is why casual smokers are effectively more hooked than heavy smokers. Not only is the illusion of pleasure greater, but they have less incentive to quit because they spend less money and are less vulnerable to the health risks.

Remember, the only pleasure smokers get is the relief from withdrawal pangs, and as I have already explained, even that pleasure is an illusion. Imagine the little nicotine monster inside your body as a permanent itch so imperceptible that most of the time you aren't even aware of it.

Now if you have a permanent itch, the natural tendency is to scratch it. As our bodies become more and more immune to nicotine the natural tendency is to chain-smoke.

There are three main factors that prevent smokers from chain-smoking:

1. MONEY. Most cannot afford to.

2. HEALTH. In order to relieve our withdrawal pangs, we have to take a poison. Capacity to cope with that poison varies with each individual and at different times and situations in his or her life. This acts as an automatic restraint.

3. DISCIPLINE. This is imposed by society, the smoker's place of employment, friends and relatives, or the smoker himself as a result of the natural tug-of-war that goes on in every smoker's mind.

I used to think of my chain-smoking as a weakness. I couldn't understand why my friends could limit their intake to ten or twenty a day. I knew I was a very strong-willed person. It never occurred to me that most smokers are incapable of chain-smoking; you need very strong lungs in order to do it. Some of these five-a-day smokers whom heavy smokers tend to envy smoke five a day because physically their constitution cannot smoke more, or because they cannot afford to smoke more, or because their job, or society, or their own hatred of being hooked won't allow them to smoke more.

Now is a good time to provide a few definitions.

THE NON-SMOKER. Someone who has never fallen for the trap, but should not be complacent. He is a non-smoker only by the grace of God. All smokers were convinced that they would never become hooked, and some non-smokers keep trying an occasional cigarette.

THE CASUAL SMOKER. There are two basic classifications of casual smokers:

1. The smoker who has fallen for the trap but doesn't realize it. Do not envy such smokers. They are merely sampling the nectar at the mouth of the pitcher plant and in all probability will soon be heavy smokers. Remember, just as all alcoholics started off as casual drinkers, so all smokers started off as casual smokers.

2. The smoker who was previously a heavy smoker and thinks he cannot stop. These smokers are the most pathetic of all.

They fall into various categories, each of which needs separate comment.

THE FIVE-A-DAY SMOKER. If he enjoys a cigarette, why does he smoke only five a day? If he can take it or leave it, why does he bother to smoke at all? Remember, the "habit" is really the banging of your head against the brick wall to make it relaxing when you stop. The five-a-day smoker is relieving his withdrawal pangs for less than one hour each day. The rest of the day, although he doesn't realize it, he is banging his head against the wall and does so for most of his life. He is smoking only five a day because either he cannot afford to smoke more or he is worried about the health risk. It is easy to convince the heavy smoker that he doesn't enjoy it, but try convincing a casual smoker. Anybody who has gone through an attempt to cut down will know it is the worst torture of all and almost guaranteed to keep you hooked for the rest of your life.

THE MORNING- OR EVENING-ONLY SMOKER. He punishes himself by suffering withdrawal pangs for half the day in order to relieve them the other half. Again, ask him why, if he enjoys a cigarette, he doesn't smoke the whole day, or if he doesn't enjoy a cigarette, why he bothers at all.

THE SIX-MONTHS-ON, SIX-MONTHS-OFF SMOKER. (Or "I can stop whenever I want to. I have done it thousands of times.") If he enjoys smoking, why does he stop for six months? If he does not enjoy it, why does he start again? The truth is he is still hooked. Although he gets rid of the physical addiction, he is left with the main problem—the brainwashing. He hopes each time that he will stop for good and soon falls for the trap again. Many smokers envy these stoppers and starters. They think, "How lucky to be able to control it like that, to smoke when you want to and stop when you want to." What they always overlook is that these stoppers and starters aren't controlling it. When they are smokers, they wish they weren't. They go through the hassle of stopping, then begin to feel deprived and fall for the trap again, then wish they hadn't. They get the worst of all worlds. When they are smokers they wish they weren't; when they are non-smokers they wish they could smoke. If you think about it, this is true all our smoking lives. When we are allowed to smoke we either take it for granted or wish we didn't. It's only when we can't have cigarettes that they appear so precious. This is the awful dilemma of smokers. They can never win because they are moping about a myth, an illusion. There is one way they can win and that is to stop smoking and stop moping!

THE "I ONLY SMOKE ON SPECIAL OCCASIONS" SMOKER. Yes, we all do to start with, but isn't it amazing how the number of occasions rapidly increase and before we know it we're smoking on all occasions?

THE "I HAVE STOPPED, BUT I HAVE AN OCCASIONAL CIGAR/CIGARETTE" SMOKER. In a way, such smokers are the saddest cases. Either they go through their lives believing they are being deprived, or more often, the occasional cigar becomes two. They remain on the slippery slope and it goes only one way— DOWNWARDS. Sooner or later they are back to being heavy smokers. They have fallen again for the very trap that they fell into in the first place.

There are two other categories of casual smoker. The first is the type who smokes just the occasional cigarette or cigar at social occasions. These people are really non-smokers. They don't enjoy smoking. It's just that they feel they are missing out. They want to be part of the action. We all start off like this. Next time the cigars go round, watch how, after a while, the smokers stop lighting those cigars. Even heavy cigarette smokers can't wait to finish them. They would much rather be smoking their own brand. The more expensive and the larger the cigar, the more frustrating it is—the damn thing seems to last all night.

The second category is very rare indeed. In fact, of all the thousands who have sought my assistance, I can think of only about a dozen examples. The type can best be described by outlining a recent case.

A woman phoned me, seeking a private session. She was a lawyer, had been smoking for about twelve years, and had never smoked more or less than two cigarettes a day in her smoking life. She was, incidentally, a very strong-willed person. I explained that the success rate in group sessions was just as high as in individual sessions, and in any event I was able to give individual therapy only if the person was so famous that it would disrupt the group. She began to cry, and I was not able to resist the tears.

The session was expensive; indeed, most smokers would wonder why she wanted to stop in the first place. They would gladly pay what I charged that woman to be able to smoke only two cigarettes a day. They make the mistake of assuming that casual smokers are happier and more in control. In control they may be, but happy they are not. In this case, both the woman's parents had died from lung cancer before she became hooked. Like me, she had a great fear of smoking before she smoked the first cigarette. Like me, she eventually fell victim to the massive pressures and tried that first cigarette. Like me, she can remember the foul taste. Unlike me, who capitulated and became a chain-smoker very quickly, she resisted the slide.

All you ever enjoy in a cigarette is the ending of the craving for it, whether it's the almost imperceptible physical craving for nicotine or the mental torture caused by not being allowed to scratch the itch. Cigarettes themselves are filth and poison. This is why you only suffer the illusion of enjoying them after a period of abstinence. Just like a hunger or thirst, the longer you suffer from it, the greater the pleasure when you finally relieve it. Smokers make the mistake of believing smoking is just a habit. They think, "If I can only keep it down to a certain level or smoke only on special occasions, my brain and body will accept it. I can then keep my smoking at that level or cut down further should I wish to." Get it clear in your mind: the "habit" doesn't exist. Smoking is drug addiction. The natural tendency is to relieve withdrawal pangs, not to endure them. Even to hold it at your current level, you would have to exercise willpower and discipline for the rest of your life because, as your body becomes immune to the drug, it wants more and more, not less and less. As the drug begins to destroy you physically and mentally, as it gradually breaks down your nervous system, your courage, and your confidence, so you are increasingly unable to resist reducing the interval between each cigarette. That is why, in the early days, we can take it or leave it. If we get a cold, we just stop. It also explains why someone like me, who never even suffered the illusion of enjoying them, had to go on chain-smoking even though every cigarette had become physical torture.

Don't envy that woman. When you smoke only one cigarette every twelve hours it appears to be the most precious thing on earth. For twelve years that poor woman had been at the center of a tug-of-war. She had been unable to stop smoking, yet was frightened to increase the intake in case she got lung cancer like her parents. But for twenty-three hours and ten minutes of every one of those days she had to fight the temptation. It took tremendous willpower to do what she did, and as I have said, such cases are rare. But it reduced her to tears in the end. Just look at it logically: either there is a genuine crutch or pleasure in smoking or there isn't. If there is, who wants to wait an hour, or a day, or a week? Why should you be denied the crutch or pleasure in the meantime? If there is no genuine crutch or pleasure, why bother to smoke at all?

I remember another case of a five-a-day man. He started the telephone conversation in a croaky voice: "Mr. Carr, I just want to stop smoking before I die." This is how that man described his life:

"I am sixty-one years old. I have cancer of the throat caused by smoking. Now I can only physically cope with five roll-ups a day.

"I used to sleep soundly through the night. Now I wake up every hour of the night and all I can think about is cigarettes. Even when I am sleeping, I dream about smoking.

"I cannot smoke my first cigarette until ten o'clock. I get up at five o'clock and make endless cups of tea. My wife gets up at about eight o'clock, and because I am so bad-tempered, she will not have me in the house. I go down to the greenhouse and try to putter about, but my mind is obsessed with smoking. At nine o'clock I begin to roll my first cigarette and I do so until it is perfect. It is not that I need it to be perfect, but it gives me something to do. I then wait for ten o'clock. When it arrives my hands are shaking uncontrollably. I do not light the cigarette then. If I do, I have to wait three hours for the next one. Eventually I light the cigarette, take one puff and extinguish it immediately. By continuing this process I can make the cigarette last one hour. I smoke it down to about a quarter of an inch and then wait for the next one."

> ❖
>
> "My skin has cleared up! There are no more dry areas on my face and no more pimples popping up! Just clean, clear, soft skin! I actually glow!! I couldn't believe it! My cheeks are actually rosy again!!!"
> —DEBBIE S.
>
> ❖

In addition to his other troubles, this poor man had burns all over his lips caused by smoking the cigarette too low. You probably have visions of a pathetic imbecile. Not so. This man was over six feet tall and an ex-sergeant in the Marines. He was a former athlete and didn't want to become a smoker. However, during World War II, society believed that cigarettes gave courage, and servicemen were issued free rations of them. This man was virtually ordered to become a smoker. He has spent the rest of his life paying through the nose, subsidizing other people's taxes, and it has ruined him physically and mentally. If he were an animal, our society would have put him out of his misery, yet we still allow mentally and physically healthy young teenagers to become hooked.

You may think the above case is exaggerated. It is extreme but not unique. There are literally thousands of similar stories. That man poured his heart out to me, but you can be sure that many of his friends and acquaintances envied him for being a five-a-day man. If you think this couldn't happen to you, STOP KIDDING YOURSELF.

IT IS ALREADY HAPPENING.

In any event smokers are notorious liars, even to themselves. They have to be. Most casual smokers smoke far more cigarettes, and on far more occasions, than they will admit to. I have had many conversations with so-called five-a-day smokers during which they have smoked more than five cigarettes in my presence. Observe casual smokers at social events such as weddings and parties. They will be chain-smoking like the best of them.

You do not need to envy casual smokers. You do not need to smoke. Life is infinitely sweeter without cigarettes.

Teenagers are generally more difficult to cure, not because they find it difficult to stop but because either they do not believe they are hooked or they are at the primary stage of the disease and suffer from the delusion that they will automatically have stopped before the secondary stage.

I would particularly like to warn parents of children who loathe smoking not to have a false sense of security. All children loathe the smell and taste of tobacco until they become hooked. You did too at one time. Also do not be fooled by government scare campaigns. The trap is the same as it always was. Children know that cigarettes kill, but they also know that one cigarette will not. At some stage they may be influenced by a girlfriend or boyfriend, school friend, or work colleague. You may think that all they need to do is try one, which will taste horrible and convince them they could never become hooked.

I find society's failure to prevent our children from becoming addicted to nicotine and other drugs to be the most disturbing facet of drug addiction. I have given much thought to this problem and have written a book called *How to Stop Your Child Smoking,* designed specifically to address the problem of how to prevent your children from becoming hooked and how to help them escape if they have already become hooked. It is a fact that the vast majority of youngsters who become dependent on heavier drugs are introduced to the concept of chemical dependency by first falling for the nicotine trap. If you can help them avoid the nicotine trap you will greatly reduce their risk of becoming dependent on heavier drugs. I beg you not to be complacent in this matter. It is necessary to protect children at the earliest possible age, and if you have a child, I strongly urge you to read that book. Even if you suspect your child might already be hooked on a drug, the book will provide excellent guidance to assist your child to escape.

CHAPTER 26

The Secret Smoker

◄○►

The secret smoker should be grouped with casual smokers, but the effects of secret smoking are so insidious that it merits a separate chapter. It can lead to the breakdown of personal relationships. In my case it nearly caused a divorce.

I was three weeks into one of my failed attempts to stop. The attempt had been triggered by my wife's worry about my constant wheezing and coughing. I had told her I was not worried about my health. She said, "I know you aren't, but how would you feel if you had to watch someone you love systematically destroying himself?" It was an argument that I found irresistible, hence the attempt to stop. The attempt ended after three weeks, following a heated argument with an old friend. It did not register until years afterwards that my devious mind had deliberately set off the argument. I felt justly aggrieved at the time, but I do not believe that it was coincidence, as I had never argued with this particular friend before, nor have I since. It was clearly the little monster at work. Anyway, I had my excuse. I desperately needed a cigarette and started smoking again.

I could not bear to think of the disappointment this would cause my wife, so I did not tell her. I just smoked when alone. Then gradually I smoked in the company of friends until it got to the point where everybody knew I was smoking except my wife. I remember being quite pleased at the time. I thought, "Well, at least it is cutting my consumption down." Eventually she accused me of continuing to smoke. I had not realized it, but she described the times I had caused an argument and stormed out of the house. At other times I had taken two hours to purchase some minor item, and on occasions when I would normally have invited her to accompany me, I had made feeble excuses to go alone.

❖

"Life is definitely a lot more enjoyable without cigarettes. The funny part is that I can't remember what it was like to smoke."
—LEE W.

❖

As the antisocial split between smokers and non-smokers widens, there are literally thousands of cases where the company of friends or relatives is restricted or avoided because of this awful weed. The worst thing about secret smoking is that it supports the fallacy in the smoker's mind that he is being deprived. At the same time, it causes a major loss of self-respect; an otherwise honest person may force himself to deceive his family and friends.

It has probably happened or is still happening to you in some form.

It happened to me several times. If you've ever watched the TV detective series *Columbo*, you know that the theme of each episode is similar. The villain, usually a wealthy and respected businessman, is convinced that he has committed the perfect murder, and his confidence in his crime remaining undetected receives a boost when he discovers that the rather shabby and unimpressive-looking Columbo is in charge of the case.

Columbo has this frustrating practice of closing the door after finishing his interrogation, having assured the suspect that he is in the clear, and before the satisfied look has disappeared from the murderer's face, Columbo reappears with: "Just one small point, sir, which I'm sure you can explain . . ." The suspect stammers, and from that point on we know and he knows that Columbo will gradually wear him down.

No matter how heinous the crime, from that point on my sympathies were with the murderer. It was almost as if I were the criminal who knew his crime would be uncovered—that's exactly how those bouts of secret smoking made me feel. The hours of not being allowed to smoke, then sneaking into the garage for a quick smoke, the ten minutes of shivering in the cold, wondering where the pleasure was. The fear of being caught red-handed. Would she discover where I'd hidden the cigarettes, lighter, and cigarette butts? The relief of returning to the house undiscovered, immediately followed by the fear that she would smell the nicotine on my breath and clothes. As I took longer and more frequent risks, the certain knowledge that sooner or later I was bound to be discovered. The final humiliation and shame when that certainty became a fact, followed by the immediate return to chain-smoking.

OH, THE JOYS OF BEING A SMOKER!

CHAPTER 27

A Social Habit?

---◄○►---

The main reason why there are more than fifteen million ex-smokers in Britain since the 1960s and even more in the United States is the social revolution that is taking place.

Yes, I know: health and money are the main reasons why we should want to stop, but then they always have been. We do not actually need cancer scares to tell us that cigarettes shatter our lives. These bodies of ours are the most sophisticated objects on the planet, and any smoker knows instantly, from the first puff, that cigarettes are poisonous.

The only reason why we ever get involved with smoking is the social pressure of our friends. The only valid "plus" smoking ever had was that it was at one time considered a perfectly acceptable social habit.

Today it is generally considered, even by smokers themselves, to be an antisocial habit.

In the old days the strong man smoked. If you didn't smoke, you were considered a sissy, and we all worked very hard to become hooked. In every bar or club the majority of men would be proudly inhaling and exhaling tobacco smoke. There would be the permanent fallout cloud, and all the ceilings that were not regularly decorated soon became yellow or brown.

Today the position is completely reversed. Today's strong man doesn't need to smoke. Today's strong man is not dependent on a drug.

With the social revolution all smokers nowadays are giving serious thought to stopping, and today's smokers are considered to be generally weak people.

The most significant trend that I have noticed since writing the first edition of this book in 1985 is the increasing emphasis on the antisocial aspect of smoking. The days when the cigarette was the proud badge of the sophisticated woman or the tough guy have gone forever. Everyone now knows that the only reason why people continue to smoke is that they have failed to stop or are too frightened to try. Every day, as the smoker is pilloried by office bans, extended bans in public places, and attacks from holier-than-thou ex-smokers, so the mannerisms of smokers are changing. I've recently seen situations that I remember witnessing as a boy but haven't seen for years—like smokers flicking ash into their hands or pockets because they are too embarrassed to ask for an ashtray.

I was in a restaurant some years ago. It was midnight. Everyone had stopped eating. At a time when the cigarettes and cigars are normally rife, not one person was smoking. I conceitedly thought, "Ah! I'm beginning to make an impression." I asked the waiter, "Is this now a non-smoking restaurant?" The reply was negative. I thought, "That's strange. I know that a lot of people are stopping, but there must be one smoker here." Eventually someone lit up in a corner, and the result was like a series of beacons going on through the restaurant. All those other smokers had been sitting there thinking, "Surely I can't be the only smoker here."

Many smokers won't smoke between courses now because they feel so self-conscious. Many not only apologize to people at the same table but also look around to see if they'll get flak from elsewhere. As every day more and more smokers leave the sinking ship, so those left on it become terrified they'll be the last.

DON'T LET IT BE YOU!

CHAPTER 28

Timing

—◀○▶—

Timing is important. Our society treats smoking flippantly as a slightly distasteful habit that can injure your health. It is not. It is drug addiction, a disease, and the number one killer in society. The worst thing that happens in most smokers' lives is getting hooked on that awful weed. If they stay hooked, horrendous things happen. Timing is important to give yourself the right to a proper cure.

First of all, identify the times or occasions when smoking appears to be important to you. If you are a businessperson and smoke for the illusion of relief of stress, pick a relatively slack period; a good idea is to choose your annual vacation. If you smoke mainly during boring or relaxing periods, do the opposite. In any event, take the matter seriously and make the attempt to stop the most important thing in your life.

Look ahead for a period of about three weeks and try to anticipate any event that might lead to failure. Occasions like a wedding or Christmas need not deter you, providing you anticipate them in advance and do not feel you will be deprived. Do not attempt to cut down in the meantime, as this will only create the illusion that the cigarette is enjoyable. In fact, it helps to force as many of the filthy things down your throat as possible. While you are smoking that last cigarette, be conscious of the bad smell and taste and think how marvelous it will be when you allow yourself to stop doing it.

WHATEVER YOU DO, DON'T FALL INTO THE TRAP OF JUST SAYING, "NOT NOW. LATER," THEN PUTTING IT OUT OF YOUR MIND. WORK OUT YOUR TIMETABLE NOW AND LOOK FORWARD TO IT. Remember you aren't giving anything up. On the contrary: you are about to receive marvelous positive gains.

For years I've been saying that I know more about the mysteries of smoking than anyone on this planet. The problem is this: although every smoker smokes purely to relieve the chemical craving for nicotine, it is not the nicotine addiction itself that hooks the smoker, but the brainwashing that results from that addiction. An intelligent person will fall for a confidence trick. But only a fool will go on falling for it once he realizes that it's a confidence trick. Fortunately, most smokers aren't fools; they only think they are. Each individual smoker has his own private brainwashing. That is why there appears to be such a wide range of different types of smoker, which only serves to compound the mysteries.

With the benefit of the years of feedback that I have had since the original publication of this book, and bearing in mind that each day I learn something new about smoking, I was agreeably surprised to realize that the philosophy I propounded in the first edition was still sound. The knowledge that I have accumulated over the years is how to better communicate that philosophy to each individual smoker. I know that every smoker can not only find it easy to stop, but can also actually enjoy the process. But that fact is pointless and exceedingly frustrating unless I can make the smoker realize it.

Many people have said to me, "You say, 'Continue to smoke until you have finished the book.' This either makes the smoker take ages to read the book or just not finish it, period. Therefore you should change that instruction." This sounds logical, but I know that if the instruction were "Stop immediately," some smokers wouldn't even start reading the book.

I had a smoker consult me in the early days. He said, "I really resent having to seek your help. I know I'm strong-willed. In every other area of my life I'm in control. Why is it that all these other smokers are stopping by their own willpower, yet I have to come to you?" He continued, "I think I could do it on my own, if I could smoke while I was doing it."

This may sound like a contradiction, but I know what the man meant. We think of stopping smoking as something that is very difficult to do. What do we need when we have something difficult to do? We need our little friend. So stopping smoking appears to be a double blow. Not only do we have a difficult task to perform, which is hard enough, but also the crutch on which we normally rely on such occasions is no longer available.

It didn't occur to me until long after the man had left that my instruction to keep smoking is the real beauty of my method. You can continue to smoke while you go through the process of stopping. You get rid of all your doubts and fears first, and when you extinguish that final cigarette you are already a non-smoker and enjoying being one.

The only chapter that has caused me to question my original advice seriously is this chapter on the matter of the right timing. Above I advise that if your special cigarette occasions are stressful situations at the office, then you should pick a holiday to make an attempt to give up, and vice versa. In fact, that isn't the easiest way to do it. The easiest way is to pick what you consider to be the most *difficult* time to do it, whether you're under stress, attending a social gathering, needing to concentrate, or just bored.

Once you've proved that you can cope with, and enjoy, life in the worst possible situation, every other situation becomes easy. But if I gave that as a definite instruction, would you even make the attempt to stop?

Let me use an analogy. My wife and I intend to swim together. We arrive at the pool at the same time, but we rarely swim together. The reason is that she immerses one toe, and half an hour later she's actually swimming. I cannot stand that slow torture. I know in advance that at some stage, no matter how cold the water is, eventually I must brave it. So I've learned to do it the easy way: I dive straight in. Now, assuming that I were in a position to insist that if she didn't dive straight in, she couldn't swim at all, I know that she wouldn't swim at all. You see the problem.

From feedback I know that many smokers have used the original advice I gave on timing to delay what they think will be the evil day. My next thoughts were to use the technique that I used for the chapter on the advantages of smoking, something like: "Timing is very important, and in the next chapter I will advise you about the best time for you to make the attempt." You turn the page over, and there is just a huge NOW.

That is, in fact, the best advice, but would you take it?

This is the subtlest aspect of the smoking trap. When we have genuine stress in our lives, it's not the time to stop, and if we have no stress in our lives, we have no desire to stop.

Ask yourself the following questions.

When you smoked that very first cigarette, did you really decide then that you would continue to smoke the rest of your life, all day, every day, without ever being able to stop?

OF COURSE YOU DIDN'T!

Are you going to continue the rest of your life all day, every day, without ever being able to stop?

OF COURSE YOU AREN'T!

So when will you stop? Tomorrow? Next year? The year after? Isn't this what you've been asking yourself since you first realized you were hooked? Are you hoping that one morning you will wake up and just not want to smoke any more? Stop kidding yourself. I waited thirty-three years for it to happen to me. With drug addiction you get progressively more hooked, not less. You think it will be easier tomorrow? You're still kidding yourself. If you can't do it today, what makes you think it will be easier tomorrow? Are you going to wait until you've actually contracted one of the killer diseases? That would be a bit pointless.

The real trap is the belief that now isn't the right time—it will always be easier tomorrow.

We believe that we live stressful lives. In fact, we don't. We've taken most genuine stress out of our lives. When you leave your home you don't live in fear of being attacked by wild animals. Most of us don't have to worry where our next meal is coming from or whether we'll have a roof over our head tonight. Just think of the life of a wild animal. Every time a rabbit comes out of its burrow, it is risking its life. But the rabbit can handle it. It's got adrenaline and other hormones—so do we. The truth is, the most stressful periods for any creature are early childhood and adolescence. But three billion years of natural selection have equipped us to cope with stress. I was five years old when World War II started. We were bombed out, and I was separated from my parents for two years. I was billeted with people who treated me unkindly. It was an unpleasant period in my life, but I was able to cope with it. I don't believe it has left me with any permanent scars; on the contrary, I believe it has made me a stronger person. When I look back on my life there has only been one thing that I couldn't handle and that was my slavery to that damned weed.

A few years ago I thought I had all the worries in the world. I was suicidal—not in the sense that I would have jumped off a roof but in the sense that I knew that smoking would soon kill me. I argued that if this was life with my crutch, life just wouldn't be worth living without it. What I didn't realize was that when you are physically and mentally depressed everything gets you down. Now I feel like a young boy again. Only one thing made the change in my life: I'm now out of the smoking pit.

I know it's a cliché to say, "If you haven't got your health, you've got nothing," but it's absolutely true. I used to think that physical-fitness fanatics like golfer Gary Player were a pain. I used to claim there's more to life than feeling fit; there's booze and tobacco. That's nonsense. When you feel physically and mentally strong you can enjoy the highs and handle the lows. We confuse responsibility with stress. Responsibility becomes stressful only when you don't feel strong enough to handle it. The Richard Burtons of this world are physically and mentally strong. What destroys them is not the stresses of life, their jobs, or old age, but the so-called crutches they turn to, which are just illusions. Sadly, in his case and for millions like him, the crutches kill.

❖

"I have tried numerous times to quit, but always failed because I felt deprived. I now feel wonderful."

—SHEILA M.

❖

Look at it this way. You've already decided that you are not going to stay in the trap the rest of your life. Therefore at some time in your life, whether you find it easy or difficult, you will have to go through the process of getting free. Smoking is not a habit or pleasure. It is drug addiction and a disease. We've already established that, far from being easier to stop tomorrow, it will get progressively harder. With a disease that's going to get progressively worse, the time to get rid of it is NOW—or as near to now as you can manage. Just think how quickly each week of our lives comes and goes. That's all it takes. Just think how nice it will be to enjoy the rest of your life without that ever-increasing black shadow hanging over you. And if you follow all my instructions, you won't even have to wait five days. You'll not only find it easy after extinguishing the final cigarette, YOU'LL ENJOY IT!

CHAPTER 29

Will I Miss the Cigarette?

N o! Once that little nicotine monster is dead and your body stops craving nicotine, any remaining brainwashing will vanish. You will find that you will be both physically and mentally better equipped not only to cope with the stresses and strains of life, but also to enjoy the good times to the fullest.

There is only one danger and that is the influence of people who are still smoking. "The other man's grass is always greener" is commonplace in many aspects of our lives and is easily understandable. Why is it in the case of smoking, where the disadvantages are so enormous compared to even the illusory "advantages," that ex-smokers tend to envy the smoker?

With all the brainwashing of our childhood it is quite understandable that we fall into the trap. Why is it that, once we realize what a fool's game it is and many of us manage to kick the habit, we walk straight back into the same trap? It is the influence of smokers.

It usually happens on social occasions, particularly after a meal. The smoker lights up and the ex-smoker has a pang. This is indeed a curious anomaly, particularly if you consider this piece of market research: not only is every non-smoker in the world happy to be a non-smoker, but every smoker in the world, even with his warped, addicted, brainwashed mind suffering the delusion that he enjoys smoking or it relaxes him, also wishes he had never become hooked in the first place. So why do some ex-smokers envy the smoker on these occasions? There are two reasons:

1. "Just one cigarette." Remember: it doesn't exist. Stop seeing that isolated occasion and start looking at it from the point of view of the smoker. You may be envying him, but he doesn't approve of himself—he envies you. Start observing other smokers. They can be the most powerful boost of all to help you quit. Notice how quickly the cigarette burns, how quickly the smoker has to light up another. Notice particularly that the smoker is not aware that he is smoking the cigarette. Even the lighting up appears to be automatic. Remember, he is not enjoying it; it's just that he cannot enjoy himself without it. Particularly remember that when he leaves your company he is going to have to go on smoking. The next morning, when he wakes up with a chest like a cesspit, he is going to have to carry on choking himself. The next time he has a pain in the chest, the next National Smoke-Out Day, the next time he inadvertently sees the government health warning, the next time there is a cancer scare, the next time he is in church, on a train, visiting a hospital, library, dentist, doctor, or supermarket, the next time he is in the company of a non-smoker, he has to continue this lifetime chain of paying through the nose just for the privilege of destroying himself physically and mentally. He is facing a lifetime of filth, bad breath, stained teeth, slavery, self-destruction, and black shadows at the back of his mind. And all of this is to achieve what purpose? The illusion of trying to get back to the state he was in before he became hooked in the first place.

2. The second reason why some ex-smokers have pangs on these occasions is that the smoker is doing something, that is, smoking a cigarette, and the non-smoker is not, so he tends to feel deprived. Get it clear in your mind before you start: it is not the non-smoker who is being deprived. It is the poor smoker who is being deprived of:

- ○ HEALTH
- ○ ENERGY
- ○ MONEY
- ○ CONFIDENCE
- ○ PEACE OF MIND
- ○ COURAGE
- ○ TRANQUILITY
- ○ FREEDOM
- ○ SELF-RESPECT

Get out of the habit of envying smokers and start seeing them as the miserable, pathetic creatures they really are. I know: I was the world's worst. That is why you are reading this book, and the ones who cannot face up to it, who have to go on kidding themselves, are the most pathetic of all.

You wouldn't envy a heroin addict. Heroin kills hundreds of people each year. Nicotine kills more than four million a year worldwide. It's already killed more people on this planet than all the wars of history combined. Like all drug addictions, yours won't get better. Each year it will get worse and worse. If you don't enjoy being a smoker today, you'll enjoy it even less tomorrow. Don't envy other smokers. Pity them. Believe me: THEY NEED YOUR PITY.

CHAPTER 30

Will I Put On Weight?

—◀○▶—

This is another myth about smoking spread mainly by smokers who, when attempting to stop on the Willpower Method, substitute sweets or other foods to help relieve withdrawal pangs. The withdrawal pangs of nicotine are very similar to hunger pangs, and the two are easily confused. However, whereas the pangs of hunger can be satisfied by food, the withdrawal pangs of nicotine are never completely satisfied.

As with any drug, after a while the body becomes immune and the drug ceases to relieve the withdrawal pangs completely. As soon as we extinguish a cigarette, the nicotine rapidly leaves our body, so that the nicotine addict has a permanent hunger. The natural inclination is eventually to chain-smoke. However, most smokers are prevented from doing this for one, or both, of two reasons.

1. Money—they cannot afford to increase their intake.

2. Health—in order to relieve the withdrawal pangs smokers have to intake a poison, which acts as an automatic check on the number of cigarettes they can smoke.

The smoker is therefore left with a permanent hunger that he can never satisfy. This is why many smokers turn to overeating, heavy drinking, or even harder drugs in order to satisfy the void. (MOST ALCOHOLICS ARE HEAVY SMOKERS. I WONDER IF IT IS REALLY A SMOKING PROBLEM?)

For the smoker the normal tendency is to start by substituting nicotine for food. During my own nightmare years I got to the stage where I cut out breakfast and lunch completely. I would chain-smoke during the day. In the later years I would actually look forward to the evenings only because then I could stop smoking. However, I would be picking at food all evening. I thought it was hunger, but it was really the withdrawal pangs from nicotine. In other words, during the day I would substitute nicotine for food and during the evenings I would substitute food for nicotine.

In those days I was twenty-eight pounds heavier than I am now and there was nothing I could do about it.

Once that little monster leaves your body, the awful feeling of insecurity ends. Your confidence returns, together with a marvelous feeling of self-respect. You obtain the assurance to take control of your life, not only in your eating habits, but also in all other ways. This is one of the many great advantages of being free from the weed.

As I have said, the weight myth is due to using substitutes during the withdrawal period. In fact, they do not make it easier to stop. They make it harder. This is explained in greater detail in a later chapter dealing with substitutes.

Provided you follow all the instructions, weight gain should not be a problem.

CHAPTER 31

Avoid False Incentives

—◄○►—

Many smokers, while trying to stop on the Willpower Method, try to increase the motivation to stop by building up false incentives.

There are many examples of this. A typical one is: "My family and I can have a wonderful vacation on the money I will save." This appears to be a logical and sensible approach, but in fact it is false because any self-respecting smoker would rather smoke fifty-two weeks in the year and not have a vacation. In any case there is doubt in the smoker's mind: not only will he have to abstain for fifty weeks, but will he even enjoy that vacation without a cigarette? All this does is to increase the sacrifice that the smoker feels he is making, which makes the cigarette even more precious in his mind. Instead concentrate on the other side: "What am I getting out of it? Why do I need to smoke?"

Another example: "I'll be able to afford a better car." That's true, and the incentive may make you abstain until you get that car, but once the novelty has gone you will feel deprived, and sooner or later you will fall for the trap again.

Another typical example is office or family pacts. These have the advantage of eliminating temptation for certain periods of the day. However, they generally fail for the following reasons:

1. The incentive is false. Why should you want to stop smoking just because other people are doing so? All this does is create an additional pressure, which increases the feeling of sacrifice. It's fine if all smokers genuinely want to stop at one particular time. However, you cannot force smokers to stop, and although all smokers secretly want to stop, until they are ready to do so a pact just creates additional pressure, which increases their desire to smoke. This turns them into secret smokers, which further increases the feeling of dependency.

2. The "rotten apple" theory, or dependency on one another. Under the Willpower Method of stopping, the smoker is undergoing a period of penance during which he waits for the urge to smoke to dissipate. If he gives in, there is a sense of failure. Under the Willpower Method one of the participants is bound to give in sooner or later. The other participants now have the excuse they have been waiting for. It's not their fault. They would have held out. It's just that Fred has let them down. The truth is that most of them have already been cheating.

3. "Sharing the credit" is the reverse of the "rotten apple" theory. Here the loss of face due to failure is not so bad when shared. There is a marvelous sense of achievement in stopping smoking. When you are doing it alone, the acclaim you receive from your friends, relatives, and colleagues can be a tremendous boost to help you over the first few days. When everybody is doing it at the same time, the credit has to be shared and the boost is consequently reduced.

Another classic example of false incentives is the bribe (such as the parent offering the teenager a sum of money to abstain or the bet, "I will give you one hundred dollars if I fail"). There was once an example on a TV program. A policeman trying to give up smoking put a twenty dollar bill in his cigarette pack. He had a pact with himself. He could smoke again, but he first had to set light to the twenty dollar bill. This stopped him for a few days, but eventually he burned the note.

Stop kidding yourself. If the $100,000 that the average smoker will spend in his lifetime, or the one-in-two risk of horrendous diseases, or the lifetime of bad breath, mental and physical torture, and slavery, or the disdain of most of the population and his own self-hatred won't stop the smoker, a few phony incentives will not make the slightest bit of difference. They will only make the sacrifice appear worse. Keep looking at the other side of the tug-of-war. Ask yourself:

What is smoking doing for me? ABSOLUTELY NOTHING.

Why do I need to do it?

YOU DON'T! YOU ARE ONLY PUNISHING YOURSELF.

CHAPTER 32

The Easy Way to Stop

—◆〈○〉◆—

This chapter contains instructions about the easy way to stop smoking. Providing you follow the instructions, you will find that stopping ranges from relatively easy to enjoyable! But remember the definition of a brunette: "a girl who didn't read the instructions on the bottle."

It is ridiculously easy to stop smoking. All you have to do is two things:

1. Make the decision that you are never going to smoke again.
2. Don't mope about it. Rejoice.

You are probably asking, "Why the need for the rest of the book? Why couldn't you have said that in the first place?" The answer is that you would at some time have moped about it, and consequently, sooner or later, you would have changed your decision. You have probably already done it many times before.

As I have already said, the whole business of smoking is a subtle, sinister trap. The main problem of stopping isn't the chemical addiction but the brainwashing, and it is necessary first to explode the myths and delusions. Understand your enemy. Know his tactics, and you will easily defeat him.

I've spent most of my life trying to stop smoking and I've suffered weeks of black depression. When I finally stopped I went from a hundred a day to zero without one bad moment. It was enjoyable even during the withdrawal period, and I have never had the slightest pang since. On the contrary, it is the most wonderful thing that has happened in my life.

I couldn't understand why it had been so easy and it took me a long time to find out the reason. It was this. I knew for certain that I was never going to smoke again. During previous attempts, no matter how determined I was, I was basically *trying* to stop smoking. I hoped that if I could survive long enough without a cigarette, the urge would eventually go. Of course it didn't go because I was waiting for something to happen, and the more I moped about it, the more I wanted a cigarette, so the craving never went.

My final attempt was different. Like all smokers nowadays, I had been giving the problem serious thought. Up to then, whenever I failed, I had consoled myself with the thought that it would be easier next time. It had never occurred to me that I would have to go on smoking the rest of my life. This latter thought filled me with horror and started me thinking very deeply about the subject.

> ❖
>
> "I finished the book ... with a feeling of 'How could I have been so stupid for so long?' I feel I've done something very positive for my future and that of my three children."
> —JOHN D.
>
> ❖

Instead of lighting up cigarettes subconsciously, I began to analyze my feelings as I was smoking them. This confirmed what I already knew. I wasn't enjoying them, and they were filthy and disgusting.

I started looking at non-smokers. Until then I had always regarded non-smokers as wishy-washy, unsociable, finicky people. However, when I examined them they appeared, if anything, stronger and more relaxed. They appeared to be able to cope with the stresses and strains of life, and they seemed to enjoy social functions more than the smokers. They certainly had more sparkle and zest than smokers.

I started talking to ex-smokers. Up to this point I had regarded ex-smokers as people who had been forced to give up smoking for health and money reasons and who were always secretly longing for a cigarette. A few did say, "You get the odd pangs, but they are so few and far between they aren't worth bothering about." But most said, "Miss it? You must be joking. I have never felt better in my life."

Talking to ex-smokers exploded another myth that I had always had in my mind. I had thought that there was an inherent weakness in me, and it suddenly dawned on me that all smokers go through this private nightmare. Basically I said to myself, "Millions of people are stopping now and leading perfectly happy lives. I didn't need cigarettes before I started, and I can remember having to work hard to get used to the filthy things. So why do I need them now?" In any event I didn't enjoy smoking. I hated the whole filthy ritual and I didn't want to spend the rest of my life being the slave of this disgusting weed.

I then said to myself: "Allen, WHETHER YOU LIKE IT OR NOT, YOU HAVE SMOKED YOUR LAST CIGARETTE."

I knew, right from that point, that I would never smoke again. I wasn't expecting it to be easy; in fact, just the reverse. I fully believed that I was in for months of black depression and that I would spend the rest of my life having the occasional pang. Instead it has been absolute bliss right from the start.

It took me a long time to work out why it had been so easy and why this time I hadn't suffered those terrifying withdrawal pangs. The reason is that they do not exist. It is the doubt and uncertainty that causes the pangs. The beautiful truth is: IT IS EASY TO STOP SMOKING. It is only the indecision and moping about it that makes it difficult. Even while smokers are addicted to nicotine, they can go for relatively long periods at certain times in their lives without bothering about it. It is only when you want a cigarette but can't have one that you suffer.

Therefore the key to making it easy is to make stopping certain and final. Not to *hope* but to *know* you have kicked it, having made the decision. Never to doubt or question it. In fact, just the reverse—always to rejoice about it.

If you can be certain from the start, it will be easy. But how can you be certain from the start unless you know it is going to be easy? This is why the rest of the book is necessary. There are certain essential points and it is necessary to get them clear in your mind before you start:

1. Realize that you can achieve it. There is nothing different about you, and the only person who can make you smoke that next cigarette is you.

2. There is absolutely nothing to give up. On the contrary, there are enormous positive gains to be had. I do not only mean you will be healthier and richer. I mean you will enjoy the good times more and be less miserable during the bad times.

3. Get it clear in your head that there is no such thing as one cigarette. Smoking is a drug addiction and a chain reaction. By moaning about the odd cigarette you will only be punishing yourself needlessly.

4. See the whole business of smoking not as a sociable habit that might injure you, but as drug addiction. Face up to the fact that, whether you like it or not, YOU HAVE GOT THE DISEASE. It will not go away because you bury your head in the sand. Remember: like all crippling diseases, it not only lasts for life but gets worse and worse. The easiest time to cure it is *now*.

5. Separate the disease (the chemical addiction) from the frame of mind of being a smoker or a non-smoker. All smokers, if given the opportunity to go back to the time before they became hooked, would jump at that opportunity. You have that opportunity today! Don't even think about it as "giving up" smoking. When you have made the final decision that you have smoked your last cigarette you will already be a non-smoker. A smoker is one of those poor wretches who have to go through life destroying themselves with cigarettes. A non-smoker is someone who doesn't. Once you have made that final decision, you have already achieved your object. Rejoice in the fact. Do not sit around moping, waiting for the chemical addiction to go. Get out and enjoy life immediately. Life is marvelous even when you are addicted to nicotine, and each day it will get better when you aren't.

The key to making it easy to quit smoking is to be certain that you will succeed in abstaining completely during the withdrawal period (maximum three weeks). If you are in the correct frame of mind, you will find it ridiculously easy.

By this stage, if you have opened your mind as I requested at the beginning, you will already have decided you are going to stop. You should now have a feeling of excitement, like a dog straining at the leash, unable to wait to get the poison out of your system.

If you have a feeling of doom and gloom, it will be for one of the following reasons:

1. Something has not gelled in your mind. Re-read the above five points, and ask yourself if you believe them to be true. If you doubt any point, re-read the appropriate sections in the book.

2. You fear failure itself. Do not worry. Just read on. You will succeed. The whole business of smoking is like a confidence trick on a gigantic scale. Intelligent people fall for confidence tricks, but it is only a fool who, having once found out about the trick, goes on kidding himself.

3. You agree with everything, but you are still miserable. Don't be! Open your eyes. Something marvelous is happening. You are about to escape from the prison.

It is essential to start with the correct frame of mind: isn't it great that I am a non-smoker!

All we have to do now is to keep you in that frame of mind during the withdrawal period, and the next few chapters deal with specific points to enable you to stay in that frame of mind during that time. After the withdrawal period you won't have to think that way. It will be automatic, and the only mystery in your life will be: "If it is so obvious, why couldn't I see it before?" However, I have two important warnings:

1. Delay your plan to extinguish your last cigarette until you have finished the book.

2. I have mentioned several times a withdrawal period of up to three weeks. This can cause misunderstanding. First, you may subconsciously feel that you have to suffer for three weeks. You don't. Secondly, avoid the trap of thinking, "Somehow I have just got to abstain for three weeks and then I will be free." Nothing will actually happen after three weeks. You won't suddenly feel like a non-smoker. Non-smokers do

not feel any different from smokers. If you are moping about stopping during the three weeks, in all probability you will still be moping about it after the three weeks. What I am saying is, if you can start right now by saying, "I am never going to smoke again. Isn't it wonderful?" after three weeks you will be completely free. Whereas if you say, "If only I can survive three weeks without a cigarette," you will be dying for a cigarette after the three weeks are up.

CHAPTER 33

The Withdrawal Period

--◀O▶--

For up to three weeks after your final cigarette you may be aware of the withdrawal pangs of nicotine. However, there is no need to suffer from them. These triggers consist of two quite separate factors:

1. The withdrawal pangs of nicotine; that empty, insecure feeling, like a hunger, which smokers experience as a craving or a need to do something with their hands.

2. The psychological trigger of certain events such as a telephone conversation.

It is the failure to understand and to differentiate between these two distinct factors that makes it so difficult for smokers to achieve success on the Willpower Method. It's also the reason why many smokers who do achieve it fall into the trap again.

Although the withdrawal pangs of nicotine cause no physical pain, do not underestimate their power. We talk of "hunger pains" if we go without food for a day; there may be "tummy rumblings," but there is no physical pain. Even so, hunger is a powerful force, and we are likely to become very irritable when deprived of food. It is similar when our body is craving nicotine. The difference is that our body needs food but it doesn't need poison, and with the right frame of mind the withdrawal pangs are easily overcome and disappear very quickly.

If smokers can abstain for a few days on the Willpower Method, the craving for nicotine soon disappears. It is the second factor that causes the difficulty. The smoker has gotten into the habit of relieving his withdrawal pangs at certain times or occasions, which causes an association of ideas (such as, "I cannot enjoy a drink without a cigarette"). It may be easier to understand the effect with the help of an example.

You have a car for a few years, and let's say the turn indicator is on the left of the steering column. On your next car it is on the right. You know it is on the right, but for a couple of weeks you put the windshield wipers on whenever you want to turn.

Stopping smoking is similar. During the early days of the withdrawal period the trigger mechanism will operate at certain times. You will think, "I want a cigarette." It is essential to counter the brainwashing right from square one; then these automatic triggers will quickly disappear. Under the Willpower Method, the smoker believes he is making a sacrifice, is moping about it, and is waiting for the urge to smoke to disappear. Rather than removing these trigger mechanisms, he is actually increasing them.

A common trigger is a meal, particularly one at a restaurant with friends. The ex-smoker is already miserable because he is being deprived of his cigarette. His friends light up and he feels even more deprived. Now he is not enjoying the meal or what should be a pleasant social occasion. Because he associates the cigarette with the meal and the social occasion he is now suffering a triple blow, and the brainwashing is actually being increased. If he is resolute and can hold out long enough, he eventually accepts his lot and gets on with his life. However, part of the brainwashing remains. One of the most pathetic things is the smoker who has given up smoking for health or money reasons, yet even after several years still craves a cigarette on certain occasions. He is pining for an illusion that exists only in his mind and is needlessly torturing himself.

Even under my method, responding to triggers is the most common failing. The ex-smoker tends to regard the cigarette as a sort of placebo or sugar pill. He thinks: "I know the cigarette does nothing for me, but if I *think* it does, on certain occasions it will be a help to me."

A sugar pill, although providing no actual physical help, can be a powerful psychological aid to relieve genuine symptoms and is therefore considered beneficial. The cigarette, however, is not a sugar pill. It creates the symptoms that it relieves and after a while ceases even to relieve these symptoms completely; the "pill" is causing the disease and, worse, happens to be the number one killer poison in society.

You may find it easier to understand the effect when related to non-smokers or a smoker who has quit for several years. Take the case of a wife who loses her husband. It is quite common at such times for a smoker, with the best intentions, to say, "Have a cigarette. It will help calm you down."

If the cigarette is accepted, it will not have a calming effect because the woman is not addicted to nicotine and there are no withdrawal pangs to relieve. At best all it will do is to give her a momentary psychological boost. As soon as the cigarette is extinguished, the original tragedy is still there. In fact, it will be increased because the woman is now suffering withdrawal pangs, and her choice is now either to endure them or to relieve them by smoking another cigarette and start the chain of misery. Again, *all* the cigarette will have done is to give a momentary psychological boost. The same effect could have been achieved by offering a word of comfort. Many non-smokers and ex-smokers have become addicted to the weed as a result of such occasions.

It is essential to counter the brainwashing right from the start. Get it quite clear in your head: you don't need the cigarette, and you are only torturing yourself by continuing to regard it as some sort of prop or boost. There is no need to be miserable. Cigarettes do not make meals or social occasions; they ruin them. Remember, too, that the smokers at that meal are not smoking because they are enjoying the cigarette. They are smoking because they have to. They are drug addicts. They cannot enjoy the meal or life without it.

Abandon the concept of the smoking habit as pleasurable in itself. Many smokers think, "If only there were a clean cigarette." Any smoker who tries herbal cigarettes soon finds out they are a waste of time. Get it clear in your mind that the only reason you have been smoking is to get the nicotine. Once you are rid of the craving for nicotine you will have no more need to stick a cigarette in your mouth than in your ear.

Whether the pang is due to actual withdrawal symptoms (the empty feeling) or a trigger mechanism, accept it. The physical pain is nonexistent, and with the right frame of mind cigarettes become no problem. Do not worry about withdrawal. The feeling itself isn't bad. It is the association with wanting a cigarette and then feeling denied that is the problem.

Instead of moping about the pang, say to yourself, "I know what it is. It's the withdrawal pang from nicotine. That's what smokers suffer all their lives and that's what keeps them smoking. Non-smokers do not suffer these pangs. It is another of the many evils of this drug. Isn't it marvelous I am purging this evil from my body!"

In other words, for the next three weeks you will have a slight trauma inside your body, but during those weeks, and for the rest of your life, something wonderful will be happening. You will be ridding yourself of an awful disease. That bonus will more than outweigh the slight trauma, and you will actually enjoy the withdrawal pangs. They will become moments of pleasure.

Think of the whole business of stopping as an exciting game. Think of the nicotine monster as a sort of tapeworm inside your stomach. You have got to starve him for three weeks, and he is going to try to trick you into lighting a cigarette to keep him alive.

At times he will try to make you miserable. At times you will be off guard. Someone may offer you a cigarette and you may forget that you have stopped. There is a slight feeling of deprivation when you remember. Be prepared for these traps in advance. Whatever the temptation, get it into your mind that it is only there because of the monster inside your body, and every time you resist the temptation you have dealt another mortal blow in the battle.

> ❖
>
> "As each day goes by, I find it harder and harder to imagine having a cigarette. I'm now beginning to experience long periods when I actually forget that I was ever a smoker."
> —DOUGLAS JAMES W.
>
> ❖

Whatever you do, don't try to forget about smoking. This is one of the things that causes smokers using the Willpower Method hours of depression. They try to get through each day hoping that eventually they'll just forget about it.

It is like not being able to sleep. The more you worry about it, the harder it becomes.

In any event you won't be able to forget about it. For the first few days the "little monster" will keep reminding you, and you won't be able to avoid it; as long as there are still smokers and extensive cigarette promotions about, you will have constant reminders.

The point is, you have no need to forget. Nothing bad is happening. Something marvelous is taking place. Even if you are thinking about it a thousand times a day, SAVOR EACH MOMENT. REMIND YOURSELF HOW WONDERFUL IT IS TO BE FREE AGAIN. REMIND YOURSELF OF THE SHEER JOY OF NOT HAVING TO CHOKE YOURSELF ANYMORE.

As I have said, you will find that the pangs become moments of pleasure, and you will be surprised how quickly you will then forget about smoking.

Whatever you do—DO NOT DOUBT YOUR DECISION. Once you start to doubt, you will start to mope, and it will get worse. Instead use the momentary pang as a boost. If it is caused by depression, remind yourself that's what cigarettes were doing to you. If you are offered one by a friend, take pride in saying, "I'm happy to say I do not need them anymore." That will hurt him, but when he sees that it isn't bothering you he will be halfway to joining you.

Remember that you had very powerful reasons for stopping in the first place. Remind yourself of all the money that one cigarette will cost you, and ask yourself whether you really want to risk those fearful diseases. Above all, remember that the feeling is only temporary and each moment is a moment nearer to your goal.

Some smokers fear that they will have to spend the rest of their lives reversing the "automatic triggers." In other words, they believe that they will have to go through life using psychological tricks to kid themselves that they don't really need a cigarette. This is not so. Remember that the optimist sees the bottle as half full and the pessimist sees it as half empty. In the case of smoking, the bottle is empty and the smoker sees it as full. It is the smoker who has been brainwashed. Once you start telling yourself that you don't need to smoke, in a very short time you won't even need to say it because the beautiful truth is . . . you do not need to smoke. It's the last thing you need to do; make sure it's not the last thing you do.

CHAPTER 34

Just One Puff

—◄○►—

The idea of "just one more puff" is the undoing of many smokers who try to stop by the Willpower Method. They will go through three or four days and then have the odd cigarette or a puff or two to tide them over. They do not realize the devastating effect this has on their morale.

For most smokers, that first puff doesn't taste good, and this gives their conscious minds a boost. They think, "Good. That wasn't enjoyable. I am losing the urge to smoke." In fact, the reverse is the case. Get it clear in your mind—CIGARETTES NEVER WERE ENJOYABLE. Enjoyment wasn't the reason why you smoked. If smokers smoked for enjoyment, they'd never smoke more than one cigarette.

The only reason you smoked was to feed that little monster. Just think: you had starved him for four days. How precious that one cigarette or just the puff must have been to him. You are not aware of it in your conscious mind, but the fix your body received will be communicated to your subconscious mind and all your sound preparation will be undermined. There will be a little voice at the back of your mind saying, "In spite of all the logic, cigarettes are precious. I want another one."

That little puff has two damaging effects.

1. It keeps the little monster alive in your body.

2. What's worse, it keeps the big monster alive in your mind. If you had the last puff, it will be easier to have the next one.

Remember: just one cigarette is how people get into smoking in the first place.

CHAPTER 35

Will It Be Harder for Me?

—◄○►—

The combinations of factors that will determine how easily each individual smoker will quit are infinite. To start with, each of us has his own character, type of work, personal circumstances, timing, and so forth.

Certain professions may make it harder than others, but providing the brainwashing is removed it doesn't have to be so. A few individual examples will help.

Quitting tends to be particularly difficult for members of the medical profession. We think it should be easier for doctors because they are more aware of the effects of ill health and see daily evidence of it. Although this supplies more forceful reasons for stopping, it doesn't make it any easier to do. The reasons are these:

1. The constant awareness of the health risks creates fear, which is one of the conditions under which we need to relieve our withdrawal pangs.

2. A doctor's work is exceedingly stressful, and he is usually not able to relieve the additional stress of withdrawal pangs while he is working.

3. He has the additional stress of guilt. He feels that he should be setting an example for the rest of the population. This puts more pressure on him and increases the feeling of deprivation.

During the doctor's hard-earned breaks, when the normal stress is momentarily relieved, that cigarette becomes very precious when used to relieve his withdrawal pangs. This is a form of casual smoking and applies to any situation where the smoker is forced to abstain for lengthy periods. Under the Willpower Method the smoker is miserable because he is being deprived. He is not enjoying the break or the cup of tea or coffee that goes with it. His sense of loss is therefore greatly increased, and because of the association of ideas, the cigarette gets credit for the total situation. However, if you can first remove the brainwashing and stop moping about the cigarette, the break and the cup of tea can still be enjoyed even while the body is craving nicotine.

Another difficult situation is boredom, particularly when it is combined with periods of stress. Typical examples are drivers or parents at home with young children. The work is stressful, yet much of the work is monotonous. During an attempt to stop on the Willpower Method a housewife, for example, has long periods in which to mope about her "loss," which increases the feeling of depression.

Again, this can be easily overcome if your frame of mind is correct. Do not worry that you are continually reminded that you have stopped smoking. Use such moments to rejoice in the fact that you are ridding yourself of the evil monster. If you have a positive frame of mind, these pangs can become moments of pleasure.

Remember, any smoker, regardless of age, sex, intelligence, or profession, can find it easy and enjoyable to stop, provided YOU FOLLOW ALL THE INSTRUCTIONS.

CHAPTER 36

The Main Reasons for Failure

—◄O►—

Th</sup>ere are two main reasons for failure. The first is the influence of other smokers. At a weak moment or during a social occasion somebody will light up. I have already dealt with
this topic at length. Use that moment to remind yourself that
there is no such thing as one cigarette. Rejoice in the fact that you
have broken the chain. Remember that the smoker envies you,
and feel sorry for him. Believe me, he needs your pity.

The other main reason for failure is having a bad day. Get it
clear in your mind before you start that, whether you are a smoker
or a non-smoker, there are good days and bad days. Life is a matter of relativity, and you cannot have ups without having downs.

The problem with the Willpower Method of stopping is that as
soon as the smoker has a bad day he starts moping for a cigarette,
and all he does is make a bad day worse. The non-smoker is better equipped, not only physically, but also mentally, to cope with
the stresses and strains of life.

If you have a bad day during the withdrawal period, just take
it on the chin. Remind yourself that you had bad days when you

smoked (otherwise you wouldn't have decided to stop). Instead of moping about it, say to yourself something like, "OK, today's not so good, but smoking is not going to cure it. Tomorrow will be better, and at least I have got a marvelous bonus at the moment. I have kicked that awful cigarette habit."

When you are a smoker you have to block your mind to the bad side of smoking. Smokers never have smokers' coughs, just permanent colds. When your car breaks down in the middle of nowhere you light a cigarette, but are you happy and cheerful? Of course you aren't. Once you stop smoking the tendency is to blame everything that goes wrong in your life on the fact that you have stopped. Now if your car breaks down, you think, "At times like these I would have lit a cigarette." That's true, but what you forget is that the cigarette didn't solve the problem, and you are simply punishing yourself by moping about an illusory crutch. You are creating an impossible situation. You are miserable because you can't have the cigarette, and you'll be even more miserable if you do. You know that you have made the correct decision by stopping smoking, so don't punish yourself by ever doubting the decision.

Remember: a positive mental approach is essential—always.

CHAPTER 37

Substitutes

—◀○▶—

Substitutes include chewing gum, sweets, peppermints, herbal cigarettes, and pills. DO NOT USE ANY OF THEM. They make it harder, not easier. If you do get a pang and use a substitute, it will prolong the pang and make it harder. What you are really saying is "I need to smoke or fill the void." It will be like giving in to a hijacker or the tantrums of a child. It will just keep the pangs coming and prolong the torture. In any event the substitutes will not relieve the pangs. Your craving is for nicotine, not food. All it will do is keep you thinking about smoking. Remember these points:

1. There is no substitute for nicotine.

2. You do not need nicotine. It is not food; it is poison. When the pangs come remind yourself that it is smokers who suffer withdrawal pangs, not non-smokers. See the pangs as another evil of the drug. See them as the death of a monster.

Remember: cigarettes create the void; they do not fill it. The quicker you teach your brain that you do not need to smoke or do anything else in its place, the sooner you will be free.

In particular, avoid any product that contains nicotine, whether it be gum, patch, nasal spray, or the latest gimmick. It is true that a small proportion of smokers who attempt to quit by using nicotine substitutes do succeed and attribute their success to such use. However, they quit in spite of the substitute and not because of it. It is unfortunate that many doctors still recommend nicotine replacement therapy (NRT).

This is not surprising because, if you don't fully understand the nicotine trap, NRT sounds very logical. It is based on the belief that when you attempt to quit smoking, you have two powerful enemies to defeat. You must:

1. Break the habit.

2. Survive the terrible physical nicotine withdrawal pains.

If you have two powerful enemies to defeat, it is sensible not to fight them simultaneously, but one at a time. So the NRT theory is that you first stop smoking but continue to take a nicotine replacement. Then, once you have broken the habit, you gradually reduce the supply of nicotine, thus tackling each enemy separately.

It sounds logical, but it is based on the wrong facts. Smoking is not habit but nicotine addiction, and the actual physical pain from nicotine withdrawal is almost imperceptible. What you are trying to achieve when you quit smoking is to kill both the little nicotine monster in your body and the big monster inside your brain as quickly as possible. All NRT does is prolong the life of the little monster, which in turn prolongs the life of the big monster.

Remember, EASYWAY makes it easy to quit immediately. You can kill the big monster (brainwashing) before you extinguish your final cigarette. The little monster will soon be dead and, even while it is dying, will be no more of a problem than it was when you were a smoker.

Just think, how can you possibly cure an addict of drug addiction by recommending the same drug? One eminent and highly respected doctor has actually stated on national television that some smokers are so dependent on nicotine that if they did quit they would have to take a nicotine substitute for life. How can a doctor get so confused as to believe that the human body is not just dependent upon food, water, and oxygen, but also on a powerful poison?

> ❖
>
> **"I didn't give up smoking; I became a non-smoker. . . . This has been the greatest achievement of my life, and I want to shout it to the world."**
> —DAVID O.
>
> ❖

We often have smokers attend our clinics who have quit smoking, but are hooked on nicotine gum. Others are hooked on the gum and are still smoking. Do not be fooled by the fact that the gum tastes awful—so did the first cigarette.

All substitutes have exactly the same effect as nicotine chewing gum. I'm now talking about this business of "I can't have a cigarette, so I'll have ordinary chewing gum, or sweets, or peppermints to help fill the void." Although the empty feeling of wanting a cigarette is indistinguishable from hunger for food, one will not satisfy the other. In fact, if anything is designed to make you want a cigarette, it's stuffing yourself with chewing gum or peppermints.

But the chief evil of substitutes is that they prolong the real problem, which is the brainwashing. By saying, "I need a substitute for smoking" what you are really saying is "I am making a sacrifice." The depression associated with the Willpower Method is caused by the fact that the smoker believes he is making a sacrifice. All you will be doing is to substitute one problem for another. There is no pleasure in stuffing yourself with sweets. You will just get fat and miserable, and in no time at all you'll be back on the weed.

Casual smokers find it difficult to dismiss the belief that they are being deprived of their little reward: the cigarette during the coffee break of office or factory workers who aren't allowed to smoke while working, or of teachers in the staff room between lessons, or the quickie by doctors between patients. Some say: "I wouldn't even take the break if I didn't smoke." That proves the point: often the break is taken, not because the smoker needs it or even wants it, but because the smoker desperately needs to scratch the itch. Remember, those cigarettes never were genuine rewards. They were equivalent to wearing tight shoes to get the pleasure of taking them off. So if you feel that you must have a little reward, let that be your substitute; while you are working, wear a pair of shoes a size too small for you, don't allow yourself to remove them until you have your break, then experience that wonderful moment of relaxation and satisfaction when you do remove them. Perhaps you feel that would be rather stupid. You are absolutely right. It's hard to visualize while you are still in the trap, but that is what smokers do. It's also hard to visualize that soon you won't need that little "reward," and you'll regard your friends who are still in the trap with genuine pity and wonder why they cannot see the point.

However, if you go on kidding yourself that the cigarette was a genuine reward or that you need a substitute to take its place, you will feel deprived and miserable, and the chances are that you'll end up smoking again. If you need a genuine break, you'll soon be enjoying that break even more because you won't have to choke yourself.

Remember, you don't need a substitute. Those pangs are a craving for poison and will soon be gone. Let that be your prop for the next few days. *Enjoy* ridding your body of poison and your mind of slavery and dependence.

If, because your appetite is better, you eat more at main meals and put on a couple of pounds during the next few days, don't worry about it. When you experience the "moment of revelation" that I describe later, you will have confidence, and you'll find that any problem you have that is capable of being solved by positive thinking you will be able to solve, including eating habits. But what you mustn't do is start picking between meals. If you do, you will get fat and miserable and you will never know when you've kicked the weed. You'll just be replacing the problem instead of getting rid of it.

CHAPTER 38

Should I Avoid Temptation Situations?

I have been categorical in my advice so far and would ask you to treat this advice as instruction rather than suggestion. I am categorical, first, because there are sound, practical reasons for my advice and, second, because those reasons have been backed up by thousands of case studies.

On the question of whether or not to try to avoid temptation during the withdrawal period, I regret that I cannot be categorical. Each smoker will need to decide for himself. I can, however, make what I hope will be helpful suggestions.

I repeat that it is fear that keeps us smoking all our lives, and this fear consists of two distinct phases:

1. How can I survive without a cigarette?

This fear is the panic that smokers experience when they are out late at night and their cigarettes begin to run out. The fear isn't caused by withdrawal pangs, but is the psychological fear of dependency—you believe you cannot survive without a cigarette. That fear actually reaches its height when you are smoking your last cigarette, at the time when your withdrawal pangs are at the lowest point.

It is the fear of the unknown, the sort of fear that people have when they are learning to dive. The diving board is one foot high but seems to be six feet high. The water is six feet deep but appears to be one foot deep. It takes courage to launch yourself. You are convinced you are going to smash your head. The launching is the hardest part. If you can find the courage to do it, the rest is easy.

This explains why many otherwise strong-willed smokers either have never attempted to stop or can survive only a few hours when they do. In fact, there are some twenty-cigarettes-a-day smokers who, when they decide to stop, actually smoke their next cigarette more quickly than if they had not decided to stop. The decision causes panic, which is stressful. This is one of the occasions when the brain triggers the instruction "Have a cigarette," but now you can't have one. You are being deprived—more stress. The trigger starts again—quickly the fuse blows and you light up.

Don't worry. That panic feeling is purely psychological and caused by the belief that you are actually dependent on nicotine. The beautiful truth is that you are not, and once that illusion is removed, so is the panic, even while the "little monster" still lives. Do not panic. Just trust me and launch yourself.

2. The second phase of fear is longer-term. It involves the fear that certain situations in the future will not be enjoyable without a cigarette or that you will not be able to cope with a trauma without the cigarette. Don't worry. If you can launch yourself you will find the opposite to be the case.

The avoidance of temptation itself falls into two main categories:

1. "I will keep my cigarettes available, although I will not smoke them. I will feel more confident knowing they are there."

I find the failure rate with people who do this to be far higher than with people who discard their cigarettes. I believe this is due mainly to the fact that if you have a bad moment during the withdrawal period, it is easy to light up a readily available cigarette. If you have the indignity of having to go out and buy a pack you are more likely to overcome the temptation, and in any event the pang will probably have passed before you get to the store.

However, I believe the main reason for the higher failure rate in these cases is that the smoker does not feel completely committed to stopping in the first place. Remember the essential to success is: CERTAINTY.

"Isn't it great that I do not need to smoke anymore?"

So, why on earth do you need cigarettes? If you still feel the need to keep cigarettes on your person, I would suggest that you re-read the book first. It means that something hasn't gelled.

2. "Should I avoid stressful or social occasions during the withdrawal period?"

My advice is, yes, try to avoid stressful situations. There is no sense in putting undue pressure on yourself.

In the case of social events my advice is the reverse. Go out and enjoy yourself right away. You do not need cigarettes even while you are still addicted to nicotine. Go to a party, and rejoice in the fact that you do not have to smoke. It will quickly prove to you the beautiful truth that life is so much better without cigarettes—and just think how much better it will be when the little monster has left your body, together with all that poison.

CHAPTER 39

The Moment of Revelation

◄○►

The moment of revelation usually takes place within three weeks after a smoker stops. The sky appears to become brighter, and instead of telling yourself you do not need to smoke, you suddenly realize that the last thread is broken and you can enjoy the rest of your life without ever needing to smoke again. This is the moment when the brainwashing ends completely. It is also usually from this point on that you start looking at other smokers as objects of pity.

Smokers using the Willpower Method do not normally experience this moment because, although they are glad to be ex-smokers, they go through life believing they are making a sacrifice.

The more you smoked, the greater this moment is, and it lasts a lifetime.

I have been very fortunate in this life and have had some wonderful moments, but the most wonderful of all was that moment of revelation. With all the other highlights of my life, although I can remember they were happy times, I can never recapture the actual feeling. I can never get over the joy of not having to smoke anymore. If ever I am feeling low and need a boost nowadays, I just think how lovely it is not to be hooked on that awful weed. Half the people who contact me after they have kicked the weed say exactly the same thing, that it was the most marvelous event of their lives. Ah! What pleasure you have to come!

With an additional twenty years' feedback, both from the book and from my consultations, I have learned that in most cases the moment of revelation occurs within a few days.

In my own case it happened before I'd extinguished my last cigarette. On many occasions in my early consulting sessions during the one-to-one period, before the end of a session smokers would say something like: "You needn't say another word, Allen. I can see it all so clearly, I know I'll never smoke again." In the group sessions I've learned to tell when it happens without individual smokers saying anything. From the letters I've received I'm also aware that it frequently happens with the book.

> ❖
>
> " ... It would still fail to express adequately how grateful I am to have been led along the correct path toward being nicotine free. ... and the sense of freedom is intoxicating."
> —EDNA J.
>
> ❖

Ideally if you follow all the instructions and understand the psychology completely, it should happen to you immediately.

Nowadays at my consultations I say to smokers that it takes about five days for the noticeable physical withdrawal to go and about three weeks for an ex-smoker to get completely free. In one way I dislike giving such guidelines. It can cause two problems. The first is that I put in people's minds the suggestion that they will have to suffer between five days and three weeks. The second is that the ex-smoker tends to think, "If I can survive for five days or three weeks, I can expect a real boost at the end of that period." However, he may have five pleasant days or three pleasant weeks, followed by one of those disastrous days that strike both non-smokers and smokers, which have nothing to do with smoking, but are caused by other factors in our lives. There our ex-smoker is, waiting for the moment of revelation, and what he experiences is depression instead. It could destroy his confidence.

If I don't give any guidelines, however, the ex-smoker can spend the rest of his life waiting for nothing to happen. I suspect that this is what happens to the vast majority of smokers who stop when using the Willpower Method.

At one time I was tempted to say that revelation should happen immediately. But if I did that and it didn't happen immediately, the ex-smoker would lose confidence and would think it was never going to happen.

People often ask me about the significance of the five days and three weeks. Are they just periods that I've drawn out of the blue? No. They are obviously not definite dates, but they reflect an accumulation of feedback over the years. About five days after stopping, the ex-smoker ceases to have smoking be the sole occupation of his mind. Most ex-smokers experience the moment of revelation around this period. What usually happens is you are in one of those stressful or social situations that once you couldn't cope with or enjoy without a cigarette. You suddenly realize that not only are you enjoying or coping with it, but the thought of having a cigarette has never even occurred to you. From that point on it is usually smooth sailing. That's when you know you are free.

I have noticed from my previous attempts using the Willpower Method, and from feedback from other smokers, that most serious attempts to stop smoking fail around the three-week period. I believe that what usually happens is that after about three weeks you sense that you have lost the desire to smoke. You need to prove this to yourself, and you light a cigarette. It tastes weird. You've proved you have kicked it. But you've also put fresh nicotine into your body, and nicotine is what your body has been craving for three weeks. As soon as you extinguish that cigarette, the nicotine starts to leave your body. Now a little voice is saying, "You haven't kicked it. You want another one." You don't light another one straight away because you don't want to get hooked again. You allow a safe period to pass. When you are next tempted you are able to say to yourself, "But I didn't get hooked again, so there's no harm in having another." You are already on your way down the slippery slope.

"I realized for the first time how much smoking really controlled my life, and I wasn't missing out at all . . ."
—DONNA B.

The key to the problem is not to wait for the moment of revelation but to realize that once you extinguish that last cigarette it is finished. You've already done all you need to do. You've cut off the supply of nicotine. No force on earth can prevent you from being free unless you mope about it or wait for revelation. Go and enjoy life; cope with it right from the start. That way you'll soon experience the moment.

CHAPTER 40

The Final Cigarette

—◄○►—

Having decided on your timing, you are now ready to smoke that last cigarette. Before you do so, check on the two essentials:

1. Do you feel certain of success?

2. Have you a feeling of doom and gloom or a sense of excitement that you are about to achieve something marvelous?

If you have any doubts, re-read the book first. Remember that you never decided to fall into the smoking trap. But that trap is designed to enslave you for life. In order to escape you need to make the positive decision that you are about to smoke your final cigarette.

Remember, the only reason that you have read this book so far is because you would dearly love to escape. So make that positive decision now. Make a solemn vow that when you extinguish that final cigarette, whether you find it easy or difficult, you will never smoke another.

Perhaps you are worried because you have made this vow several times in the past but are still smoking, or you fear that you will have to go through some awful trauma. Have no fear—the worst thing that can possibly happen is that you fail, and so you have absolutely nothing to lose and so much to gain.

But stop even thinking about failure. The beautiful truth is that it is ridiculously easy to quit and you can actually enjoy the process. This time you are going to use EASYWAY! All you need to do is to follow the simple instructions that I'm about to give you:

1. Make the solemn vow now and mean it.

2. Smoke that final cigarette consciously, inhale the filth deeply into your lungs, and ask yourself where the pleasure is.

3. When you extinguish it, do so not with a feeling of "I must never smoke another," or "I'm not allowed to smoke another," but with the feeling of "Isn't it great! I'm free! I'm no longer the slave of nicotine! I don't ever have to put these filthy things in my mouth again."

4. Be aware that for a few days, there will be a little nicotine saboteur inside your stomach. You might only know the feeling "I want a cigarette." At times I refer to that little nicotine monster as the slight physical craving for nicotine. Strictly this is incorrect, and it is important that you understand why. Because it takes about three weeks for that little monster to die, ex-smokers believe that the little monster will continue to crave cigarettes after the final cigarette has been extinguished and that they must therefore use willpower to resist the temptation during this period. This is not so. The body doesn't crave nicotine. Only the brain craves nicotine. If you do get that feeling of "I want a cigarette" over the next few days, your brain has a simple

choice. It can interpret that feeling for what it actually is—an empty insecure feeling started by the first cigarette and perpetuated by every subsequent one. Now you can rejoice and say to yourself: YIPPEE, I'M A NON-SMOKER!

Or you can start the craving for a cigarette and suffer it for the rest of your life. Just think for a moment. Wouldn't that be an incredibly stupid thing to do? To say, "I never want to smoke again," then spend the rest of your life saying, "I'd love a cigarette." That's what smokers who use the Willpower Method do. No wonder they feel so miserable. They spend the rest of their lives desperately moping about something they desperately hope they will never have. No wonder so few of them succeed and the few that do never feel completely free.

5. It is only the doubting and the waiting that make it difficult to quit. So never doubt your decision; you know it's the right one. If you begin to doubt it, you will put yourself in a no-win situation. You will be miserable if you crave a cigarette but can't have one. You will be even more miserable if you do have one. No matter what system you are using, what is it that you are trying to achieve when you quit smoking? Never to smoke again? No! Many ex-smokers do that but go through the rest of their lives feeling deprived. What is the real difference between smokers and non-smokers? Non-smokers have no need or desire to smoke; they do not crave cigarettes and do not need to exercise willpower in order not to smoke. That's what you are trying to achieve, and it is completely within your power to achieve it. You don't have to wait to stop craving cigarettes to become a non-smoker. You do it the moment you extinguish that final cigarette; you have cut off the supply of nicotine: YOU ARE ALREADY A HAPPY NON-SMOKER!!!

And you will remain a happy non-smoker provided:

1. You never doubt your decision.

2. You don't wait to become a non-smoker. If you do, you will merely be waiting for nothing to happen, which will create a phobia.

3. You don't wait for the "moment of revelation" to come or try not to think about smoking. Either way you will merely create a phobia.

4. You don't use substitutes.

5. You see all other smokers as they really are and pity them rather than envy them.

6. Whether you have good days or bad days, you don't change your life just because you've quit smoking. If you do you will be making a genuine sacrifice and there is no need to. Remember, you haven't given up living. You haven't given up anything. On the contrary, you've cured yourself from an awful disease and escaped from an insidious prison. As the days go by and your health, both physical and mental, improves, the highs will appear higher and the lows less low than when you were a smoker.

7. Whenever you think about smoking, either during the next few days or the rest of your life, you think: YIPPEE, I'M A NON-SMOKER!!!

CHAPTER 41

A Final Warning

—◄○►—

No smoker, given the chance of going back to the time before he became hooked, with the knowledge he has now, would opt to start. Many of the smokers who consult me are convinced that if I could only help them stop, they would never dream of smoking again. Yet, thousands of smokers successfully kick the habit for many years and lead perfectly happy lives, only to get trapped once again.

I trust that this book will help you find the easy way to stop smoking. But be warned: smokers who find it easy to stop find it easy to start again.

DO NOT FALL FOR THIS TRAP.

No matter how long you have stopped or how confident you are that you will never become hooked again, make it a rule of life not to smoke for any reason. Resist the millions of dollars that the tobacco companies spend on promotion, and remember, they are pushing the number one killer drug and poison. You wouldn't be tempted to try heroin; yet cigarettes kill hundreds of thousands more people than heroin does.

Remember, that first cigarette will do nothing for you. You will have no withdrawal pangs to relieve, and it will taste awful. What it will do is put nicotine into your body, and a little voice at the back of your mind will start saying, "I want another one." Then you have the choice of being miserable for a while or starting the whole filthy chain again.

CHAPTER 42

Twenty Years' Feedback

—◀◎▶—

Since the original publication of this book I now have twenty years' feedback, both from my own consultations and from the book itself. Originally my efforts to spread the word were a struggle. My method was pooh-poohed by the so-called experts. Now smokers fly in from all over the world to attend my consultations, and more members of the medical profession attend them than members of any other profession. The book is already regarded in Britain as the most effective aid for stopping smoking, and its reputation is rapidly spreading throughout the rest of the world.

I'm not a do-gooder. I wage my war—which, I emphasize, is not against smokers but against the nicotine trap— for the purely selfish reason that I enjoy it. Every time I hear of a smoker escaping from the prison I get a feeling of great pleasure, even when it has nothing to do with me. You can also imagine the immense pleasure I obtain from the thousands of grateful letters that I have received over the years.

There has also been considerable frustration. The frustration is caused mainly by two categories of smoker. First, in spite of the warning in the previous chapter, I am disturbed by the number of smokers who find it easy to stop, yet get hooked again and find they can't succeed the next time. This applies not only to smokers who read the book but also to those who attend my consultations.

A man telephoned me a few years ago. He was very distraught; in fact, he was crying. He said, "I'll pay you one thousand pounds if you can help me stop for a week. I know if I can just survive a week, I'll be able to do it." I told him that I charge a fixed fee and that was all he need pay. He attended a group session and, much to his surprise, found it easy to stop. He sent me a very nice thank-you letter.

Practically the last thing I say to ex-smokers leaving my sessions is: "Remember, you must never smoke another cigarette." This particular man said, "Have no fear, Allen. If I manage to stop, I'll definitely never smoke again."

I could tell that the warning hadn't really registered. I said, "I know you feel like that at the moment, but how will you feel six months on?"

He said, "Allen, I will never smoke again."

About a year later there was another phone call. "Allen, I had a small cigar at Christmas, and now I'm back on forty cigarettes a day."

I said, "Do you remember when you first phoned? You hated it so much you were going to pay me one thousand pounds if you could stop for a week."

"I remember. Haven't I been stupid?"

"Do you remember you promised me you would never smoke again?"

"I know. I'm a fool."

It's like finding someone up to his neck in a bog and about to go under. You help pull him out. He is grateful to you and then, six months later, dives straight back into the bog.

Ironically, when this man attended a subsequent session he said, "Can you believe it? I offered to pay my son a thousand pounds if he hadn't smoked by his twenty-first birthday. I paid up. He's now twenty-two and puffing away like a chimney. I can't believe he could be so stupid."

I said, "I don't see how you can call him stupid. At least he avoided the trap for twenty-two years, and he doesn't know the misery he's in for. You knew it as well as anyone and survived only a year."

Smokers who find it easy to stop and start again pose a special problem. However, when you get free, PLEASE, PLEASE, DON'T MAKE THE SAME MISTAKE.

Smokers believe that such people start again because they are still hooked and are missing the cigarette. In fact, they find stopping so easy that they lose their fear of smoking. They think, "I can have an odd cigarette. Even if I do get hooked again, I'll find it easy to stop again."

I'm afraid it just doesn't work that way. It's easy to stop smoking, but it's impossible to try to control the addiction. The one thing that is essential to becoming a non-smoker is *not to smoke*.

The second category of smokers that causes me frustration consists of those who are just too frightened to make the attempt to stop or, when they do, find it a great struggle. The main difficulties appear to be the following:

1. Fear of failure. There is no disgrace in failure, but not to try is plain stupidity. Look at it this way—you're hiding from nothing. The worst thing that can happen is that you fail, in which case you are no worse off than you are now. Just think how wonderful it would be to succeed. If you don't make the attempt, you have already guaranteed failure.

2. Fear of panic and of being miserable. Don't worry about it. Just think: what awful thing could happen to you if you never smoked another cigarette? Absolutely nothing. Terrible things will happen if you do keep smoking. In any case, the panic is

caused by cigarettes and will soon be gone. The greatest gain is to be rid of that fear. Do you really believe that smokers are prepared to have their arms and legs removed for the pleasure they get from smoking? If you find yourself feeling panicky, deep breathing will help. If you are with other people and they are getting you down, get away from them. Escape to the garage or an empty office or wherever.

If you feel like crying, don't be ashamed. Crying is nature's way of relieving tension. No one has ever had a good cry without feeling better afterwards. One of the awful things we do to young boys is to teach them not to cry. You see them trying to fight the tears back, but watch the jaw grinding away. In Britain, they teach us to "keep a stiff upper lip," not to show any emotions. We are *meant* to show emotions, not to try to bottle them up inside us. Scream or shout or have a tantrum. Kick a cardboard box or filing cabinet. Regard your struggle as a boxing match that you cannot lose.

No one can stop time. Every moment that passes, that little monster inside you is dying. Enjoy your inevitable victory.

3. Not following the instructions. Incredibly, some smokers say to me, "Your method just didn't work for me." They then describe how they ignored not just one instruction, but practically all of them. (For clarification I will summarize these in the checklist at the end of the chapter.)

4. Misunderstanding instructions. The chief problems appear to be these:

   ○ "I can't stop thinking about smoking." Of course you can't, and if you try, you will create a phobia and be miserable. It's like trying to get to sleep at night; the more you try, the harder it becomes. I think about smoking ninety percent of my life. It's *what* you are thinking that's important. If you are thinking, "Oh, I'd love a cigarette," or "When will I be free?" you'll be miserable. If you are thinking, "YIPPEE! I am free!" you'll be happy.

○ "When will the little physical monster die?" The nicotine leaves your body very rapidly. But it is impossible to tell when your body will cease to suffer from the slight physical sensation of nicotine withdrawal. That empty, insecure feeling is identical to normal hunger, depression, or stress. All the cigarette does is increase the level of it. This is why smokers who stop by using the Willpower Method are never quite sure whether they've kicked it. Even after the body has ceased to suffer from nicotine withdrawal, if they suffer normal hunger or stress, their brain is still saying, "That means you want a cigarette." The point is we don't have to wait for the nicotine craving to disappear; it is so slight that we don't even know it's there. We know it only as feeling "I want a cigarette." When you leave the dentist after the final session, do you wait for your jaw to stop aching? Of course you don't. You get on with your life. Even though your jaw's still aching, you are elated.

○ Waiting for the moment of revelation. If you wait for it, you are just causing another phobia. I once stopped for three weeks on the Willpower Method. I met an old school friend and ex-smoker. He said, "How are you getting on?"
I said, "I've survived three weeks."
He said, "What do you mean, you've survived three weeks?"
I said, "I've gone three weeks without a cigarette."
He said, "What are you going to do? *Survive* the rest of your life? What are you waiting for? You've done it. You're a non-smoker."

I thought, "He's absolutely right. What am I waiting for?" Unfortunately, because I didn't fully understand the nature of the trap at that time, I was soon back in it, but the point was noted. You become a non-smoker when you extinguish your last cigarette. The important thing is to be a happy non-smoker from the start.

○ "I am still craving cigarettes." Then you are being very stupid. How can you claim, "I want to be a non-smoker," and then say, "I want a cigarette"? That's a contradiction. If you say, "I want a cigarette," you are saying, "I want to be a smoker." Non-smokers don't want to smoke cigarettes. You already know what you really want to be, so stop punishing yourself.

○ "I've opted out of life." Why? All you have to do is stop choking yourself. You don't have to stop living. Look, it's as simple as this. For the next few days you'll have a slight trauma in your life. Your body will suffer the almost imperceptible aggravation of withdrawal from nicotine. Now, bear this in mind: you are no worse off than you were. This is what you have been suffering the whole of your smoking life, every time you have been asleep or in a church, supermarket, or library. It didn't seem to bother you when you were a smoker, and if you don't stop, you'll go on suffering this distress for the rest of your life. Cigarettes don't make meals or drinks or social occasions; they ruin them. Even while your body is still craving nicotine, meals and social occasions are marvelous. Life is marvelous. Go to social functions, even if there are twenty smokers there. Remember that *you* are not being deprived; *they* are. Every one of them would love to be in your position. Enjoy being the prima donna and the center of attention. Stopping smoking is a wonderful conversation point, particularly when smokers see that you are happy and cheerful. They'll think that you are incredible. The important point is that you'll be enjoying life right from the start. There's no need to envy them. They'll be envying you.

○ "I am miserable and irritable." That is because you haven't followed one of my instructions. Find out which one it is. Some people understand and believe everything I say, but still start off with a feeling of doom and gloom, as if something terrible were happening. You are doing not only what you'd like to do, but what every smoker on the planet would like to do. With any method of stopping, what the ex-smoker is trying to achieve is a certain frame of mind so that whenever he thinks about smoking he says to himself, "YIPPEE! I'M FREE!" If that's your object, why wait? Start off in that frame of mind and never lose it. The rest of the book is designed to make you understand why there is no alternative.

THE CHECKLIST

If you follow these simple instructions, you cannot fail.

1. Make a solemn vow that you will never, ever, smoke, chew, or suck anything that contains nicotine, and stick to your vow.

2. Get this clear in your mind: there is absolutely nothing to *give up*. By that I don't mean simply that you will be better off as a non-smoker (you've known that all your life); nor do I mean that although there is no rational reason why you smoke, you must get some form of pleasure or crutch from it or you wouldn't do it. What I mean is, there is no genuine pleasure or crutch in smoking. It is just an illusion, like

banging your head against a wall to make it pleasant when you stop.

3. There is no such thing as a confirmed smoker. You are just one of the millions who have fallen for this subtle trap. Like millions of other ex-smokers who once thought they couldn't escape, you have escaped.

4. If at any time in your life you were to weigh the pros and cons of smoking, the conclusion would always be, a dozen times over, "Stop doing it. You are a fool." Nothing will ever change that. It always has been that way, and it always will be. Having made what you know to be the correct decision, don't ever torture yourself by doubting it.

5. Don't try *not* to think about smoking or worry that you are thinking about it constantly. But whenever you do think about it—whether it be today, tomorrow, or the rest of your life—think, "YIPPEE! I'M A NON-SMOKER!"

6. DO NOT use any form of substitute.
   DO NOT keep your own cigarettes.
   DO NOT avoid other smokers.
   DO NOT change your lifestyle in any way purely because you've stopped smoking.
   If you follow the above instructions, you will soon experience the moment of revelation. But:

7. Don't wait for that moment to come. Just get on with your life. Enjoy the highs and cope with the lows. You will find that in no time at all the moment will arrive.

CHAPTER 43

Help the Smoker Left on the Sinking Ship

—◀○▶—

Smokers are panicking nowadays. They sense that there is a change in society. Smoking is now regarded as an unsociable habit, even by smokers themselves. They also sense that the whole thing is coming to an end. Millions of smokers are now stopping, and all smokers are conscious of this fact.

Every time a smoker leaves the sinking ship, the ones left on it feel more miserable. Every smoker instinctively knows that it is ridiculous to pay good money for dried leaves rolled up in paper, to set light to them, and to breathe cancer-triggering tar into his lungs. If you still don't think it is silly, try sticking a burning cigarette in your ear and ask yourself what the difference is. Just one. You cannot get the nicotine that way. If you can stop sticking cigarettes in your mouth, you won't need the nicotine.

Smokers cannot find a rational reason for smoking, but if someone else is doing it, they do not feel quite so silly.

Smokers blatantly lie about their habit, not only to others, but to themselves. They have to. The brainwashing is essential if they are to retain some self-respect. They feel the need to justify their habit, not only to themselves, but to non-smokers. They are therefore forever advertising the illusory advantages of smoking.

If a smoker stops on the Willpower Method, he still feels deprived and tends to become a moaner. All this does is to confirm to other smokers how right they are to keep smoking.

If the ex-smoker succeeds in kicking the habit, he is grateful that he no longer has to go through life choking himself or wasting money. But he has no need to justify himself; he doesn't sit there saying how marvelous it is not to be smoking. He will do that only if he is asked, and smokers won't ask that question. They wouldn't like the answer. Remember, it is fear that keeps them smoking, and they would rather keep their heads in the sand.

The only time they ask that question is when it is time to stop.

Help the smoker. Remove these fears. Tell him how wonderful it is not to have to go through life choking yourself, how lovely it is to wake up in the morning feeling fit and healthy instead of wheezing and coughing, how wonderful it is to be free of slavery, to be able to enjoy the whole of life, to be rid of those awful black shadows. Or, better still, get him to read this book.

It is essential not to belittle the smoker by indicating that he is polluting the atmosphere or is in some way unclean. There is a common conception that the ex-smoker is the worst in this respect. I believe this conception has some substance, and I think this is due to the Willpower Method of stopping. Although the ex-smoker has kicked the habit, he retains some of the brainwashing, and part of him therefore still believes that he has made a sacrifice. He feels vulnerable, and his natural defense mechanism is to attack the smoker. This may help the ex-smoker, but it does nothing to help the smoker. All it does is make him feel even more wretched and consequently make his need for a cigarette even greater.

Although the change in society's attitude to smoking is the main reason why millions of smokers are quitting, it doesn't make it easier for them to do so. In fact, it makes it a great deal harder. Most smokers nowadays believe they are stopping mainly for health reasons. This is not strictly true. Although the enormous health risk is obviously the chief reason for quitting, smokers have been killing themselves for years and it has made not the slightest difference. The main reason why smokers are stopping is because society is beginning to see smoking for what it actually is: filthy drug addiction. The enjoyment was always an illusion; this attitude removes this illusion, so that the smoker is left with nothing.

The complete ban on smoking in many subway systems is a classic example of the smoker's dilemma. The smoker either takes the attitude: "OK, if I cannot smoke on the train, I will find another means of travel," which does no good, or he says: "Fine, it will help me cut down on my smoking." The result of this is that instead of smoking one or two cigarettes on the train, neither of which he would have enjoyed, he abstains for an hour. During this enforced period of abstinence, however, not only will he be mentally deprived and waiting for his reward, but his body will also have been craving nicotine—and oh, how precious that cigarette will be when he is eventually allowed to light up.

Enforced abstinence does not actually cut down the intake because the smoker just indulges in more cigarettes when he is eventually allowed to smoke. All it does is ingrain in the smoker's mind how precious cigarettes are and how dependent he is upon them.

I think the most insidious aspect of this enforced abstinence is its effect on pregnant women. We allow teenaged girls to be bombarded with massive advertising that gets them hooked in the first place. Then, during pregnancy, one of the most stressful periods in women's lives, when in their deluded minds they need cigarettes most of all, the medical profession blackmails them into giving up because of the harm they are causing the baby. Many are unable to do so and are forced, through no fault of their own, to suffer a guilt complex for the rest of their lives. Many of them succeed and are pleased to do so, thinking, "Fine, I will do this for the baby and after nine months I will be cured anyway." Then comes the pain and fear of labor, followed by the biggest "high" of their lives. The pain and fear are over, and the beautiful, new baby has arrived—and the old trigger mechanism comes into operation. Part of the brainwashing is still there, and almost before the cord has been cut, the woman has a cigarette in her mouth. The elation of the birth blocks the foul taste from her mind. She has no intention of becoming hooked again. "Just the one cigarette." Too late! She is already hooked. Nicotine has gotten into her body again. The old craving will start, and even if she does-

❖

"My life at the moment is one big miracle! Everything feels new and fantastic. You opened the door for me to walk through, and I can't thank you enough!"
—DEBBIE S.

❖

n't become hooked right away, postnatal depression will probably get her smoking again.

It is strange that although heroin addicts are criminals according to law, our society's attitude is "What can we do to help the pathetic individuals?" Let us adopt the same attitude to the poor smoker. He is not smoking because he wants to, but because he thinks he has to, and unlike the heroin addict, he usually has to suffer years and years of mental and physical torture. We always say a quick death is better than a slow one, so do not envy the poor smoker. He deserves your pity.

CHAPTER 44

Advice to Non-Smokers

—◄○►—

HELP GET YOUR SMOKING FRIENDS OR RELA-
TIVES TO READ THIS BOOK. First study the con-
tents of this book and try to put yourself in the place of the
smoker.

Do not force him to read this book or try to stop him smoking
by telling him he is ruining his health or wasting his money. He
already knows this better than you do. Smokers do not smoke because they enjoy it or because they want to. They only tell themselves and other people this in order to retain self-respect. They
smoke because they feel dependent on cigarettes, because they
think that the cigarette relaxes them and gives them courage and
confidence and that life will never be enjoyable without a cigarette. If you try to force a smoker to stop, he feels like a trapped
animal and wants his cigarette even more. This may turn him into
a secret smoker, and in his mind the cigarette will become even
more precious (see chapter 26).

Instead, concentrate on the other side of the coin. Get him
into the company of ex-smokers (there are currently more than

nine million of them in Britain alone and many more in the U.S.). Get the ex-smokers to tell the smoker how they, too, thought they were hooked for life and how much better life is as a non-smoker.

Once you have him believing that he can stop, his mind will start opening. Then start explaining the delusion created by withdrawal pangs. Not only are the cigarettes failing to give him a boost, but they are also destroying his confidence and making him irritable and unrelaxed.

He should now be ready to read this book himself. He will be expecting to read pages and pages about lung cancer, heart disease, and the

"I had to read the book three times before the penny dropped! Now I've got my life back. You are a genius!!!!!"
—CUFF E.

like. Explain that the approach is completely different and that references to illness are just a small fraction of the material in the book.

HELP DURING THE WITHDRAWAL PERIOD. Whether the ex-smoker is suffering or not, assume that he is. Do not try to minimize his suffering by telling him it is easy to stop; he can do that himself. Instead keep telling him how proud you are, how much better he is looking, how much sweeter he smells, how much easier his breathing is. It is particularly important to keep doing this. When a smoker makes an attempt to stop, the euphoria of the attempt and the attention he gets from friends and colleagues can help him along. However, they tend to forget quickly, so keep that praise going.

Because he is not talking about smoking, you may think he has forgotten about it and it's best not to remind him. Usually the complete opposite is the case with the Willpower Method, as the ex-smoker tends to be obsessed by nothing else. So do not be frightened to bring the subject up, and keep praising him; he will tell you if he doesn't want you to remind him of smoking.

Go out of your way to relieve him of pressures during the withdrawal period. Try to think of ways of making his life interesting and enjoyable.

This can also be a trying period for non-smokers. If one member of a group is irritable, it can cause general misery all around. So anticipate this if the ex-smoker is feeling irritable. He may well take it out on you, but do not retaliate; it is at this time that he needs your praise and sympathy the most. If you are feeling irritable yourself, try not to show it.

One of the tricks I used to play when trying to give up with the aid of the Willpower Method was to get into a tantrum, hoping that my wife or friends would say, "I cannot bear to see you suffering like this. For goodness' sake, have a cigarette." The smoker then does not lose face, as he hasn't "given in"—he's been instructed. If the ex-smoker uses this ploy, on no account encourage him to smoke. Instead say, "If that is what cigarettes do to you, thank goodness you will soon be free. How marvelous that you had the courage and sense to give up."

Finale: Help End This Scandal

—◀○▶—

I n my opinion, cigarette smoking is the biggest scandal in society, even more so than nuclear weapons.

Surely the very basis of civilization, the reason why the human species has advanced so far, is that we are capable of communicating our knowledge and experiences not only to each other, but also to future generations. Even other species find it necessary to warn their offspring of the pitfalls in life.

If nuclear weapons do not go off, there is no problem. The people who advocate nuclear armament can carry on saying smugly, "The weapons are keeping the peace." If they do go off, they will solve the smoking problem and every other problem, and a bonus for the politicians is that there will be nobody around to say, "You were wrong" (I wonder if this is why they support nuclear weapons).

However, much as I disagree with nuclear weapons, at least such decisions are made in good faith, in the genuine belief that they help mankind, whereas with smoking, the true facts are known. Maybe during World War II people genuinely believed that cigarettes provided courage and confidence. Today the authorities know that is a fallacy. Look at the cigarette advertisements nowadays. They make claims about the quality of the tobacco. Why should we be worried about the quality of a poison?

215

The sheer hypocrisy is incredible. As a society we get uptight about glue sniffing and heroin addiction. Compared with cigarette smoking, these problems are mere pimples in our society. As of 2002, about twenty-two percent of the American population and twenty-six percent of the British population were addicted to nicotine, and most of them spend the bulk of their pocket money on cigarettes. Tens of thousands of people have their lives ruined every year because they become hooked. Smoking is by far the biggest killer in society and yet the biggest vested interest is the British treasury. It makes eight billion pounds every year out of the misery of nicotine addicts, and the tobacco empires are allowed to spend millions per year advertising the filth.

How clever that cigarette companies print health warnings on packs, and the British government spends a pittance on TV campaigns involving cancer scares, bad breath, and legs being chopped off, and then they justify themselves morally by saying, "We have warned you of the danger. It is your choice." The smoker doesn't have the choice anymore than the heroin addict does. Smokers do not decide to become hooked; they are lured into a subtle trap. If smokers had the choice, the only smokers tomorrow morning would be the youngsters starting out believing they could stop anytime they wanted to.

Why the phony standards? Why are heroin addicts seen as criminals, yet able to register as addicts in England and get free heroin and proper medical treatment to help get off it? Just try registering as a nicotine addict. You cannot get cigarettes at cost. You have to pay three times the true value.

If you go to your doctor for help, either he will tell you, "Stop doing it, it's killing you," which you already know, or he will prescribe another form of nicotine addiction that will cost you a prescription fee and actually contains the drug you are trying to kick.

Scare campaigns do not help smokers stop. They make it harder. All they do is frighten smokers, which makes them want to smoke even more. They don't even prevent teenagers from becoming hooked. Teenagers know that cigarettes kill, but they also know one cigarette will not do it. Because the habit is so prevalent, sooner or later the teenager, through social pressures or curiosity, will try just one cigarette. And *because* it tastes so awful, he will probably become hooked.

Why do we allow this scandal to go on? Why don't governments come out with proper campaigns? Why don't they tell us that nicotine is a drug and a killer poison, that it does not relax you or give you confidence but destroys your nerves, and that it can take just one cigarette to become hooked?

I remember reading H.G. Wells's *The Time Machine*. The book describes an incident in the distant future in which a man falls into a river. His companions merely sit around the bank like cattle, oblivious to his cries of desperation. I found that incident inhuman and very disturbing. I find the general apathy of our society to the smoking problem very similar. In England, darts tournaments sponsored by tobacco companies are televised during peak viewing hours. There is a cry of "One hundred and eighty." The player is then shown lighting a cigarette. Imagine the furor if the tournament were being sponsored by the Mafia and the player were a heroin addict, shown injecting himself.

Why do we allow society to subject healthy young teenagers, whose lives are complete before they start smoking, to pay through the nose for the rest of their lives just for the privilege of destroying themselves mentally and physically in a lifetime of slavery, a lifetime of filth and disease?

You may feel that I overdramatize the facts. Not so. My father was cut down in his early fifties because of cigarette smoking. He was a strong man and might still have been alive today if he'd never smoked.

I believe I was within an inch of dying during my forties, although my death would have been attributed to a brain hemorrhage rather than to cigarette smoking. I now spend my life being consulted by people who have been crippled by the disease or are in the last stages. And, if you care to think about it, you probably know of many, too.

There is a wind of change in society. A snowball has started that I hope this book will help turn into an avalanche.

You, too, can help by spreading the message.

FINAL WARNING

You can now enjoy the rest of your life as a happy non-smoker. In order to make sure that you do, you need to follow these simple instructions:

1. Keep this book safely in a place where you can easily refer to it. Do not lose it, lend it, or give it away.

2. If you ever start to envy another smoker, realize that he or she will be envious of you. You are not being deprived. The smoker is.

3. Remember you did not enjoy being a smoker. That's why you stopped. You do enjoy being a non-smoker.

4. Remember, there is no such thing as just one cigarette.

5. Never doubt your decision never to smoke again. You know it's the correct decision.

Now at last you can say
"YIPPEE! I'M A NON-SMOKER"

You have achieved something really marvelous. Every time I hear of a smoker escaping from the sinking ship, I get a feeling of enormous satisfaction.

It would give me great pleasure to hear that you have freed yourself from the slavery of the weed. Please sign the letter and add your comments, and send it back to:

Allen Carr USA
1133 Broadway, Suite 706
New York, NY 10010
Tel: (212) 696-6768 or toll-free 1-866-NO NIC 99 (666-4299)
E-mail: feedback@allencarrusa.com

YIPPEE! I'M A NON-SMOKER

Signed   Date

Name

Address

                       Zip Code

Comments

ALLEN CARR'S EASYWAY™ CLINICS–U.S.A.

Allen Carr has its North American Headquarters in New York. Our clinics are currently operational throughout the United States and in major cities across Canada.

Sessions last around five hours and are held in groups of up to thirty smokers. We offer all attendees a money-back guarantee, a copy of which is posted on our website www.allencarrusa.com

Based on our unique money-back guarantee the success rate at Allen Carr's seventy clinics worldwide has been over ninety percent for the past twenty years.

For more information about clinics in your area or to make a booking, please call toll-free: **1 866 NO NIC 99 (666 4299)**

Some cell phone users cannot call toll-free numbers. If you cannot reach us on the toll-free line please call our **New York** office at **(212) 330-9194**. Alternatively, feel free to visit **www.allencarr.com** or e-mail us at **reservations@allencarrusa.com**

At our Web site, in addition to information about the clinics, you will also find our Bulletin Board, which offers online support and chat, and the Allen Carr Newsletter, which provides up-to-date information about the expansion of the USA Clinic Network and developments in other areas.

We welcome all comments and feedback about the Allen Carr method. Please feel free to share your experiences with us.

Letters can be sent to our NY office:

Allen Carr USA

1133 Broadway, Suite 706

New York, NY 10010

Alternatively, please e-mail any comments or feedback to **feedback@theeasywaytostopsmoking.com**.

ALLEN CARR'S EASYWAY™ CLINICS—WORLDWIDE

The following pages list contact details for all Allen Carr's Easyway to Stop Smoking Clinics and Centers worldwide where the success rate, based on the three-month money back guarantee, is over ninety percent. Selected clinics also offer sessions that deal with alcohol and weight issues. Please check with your nearest clinic, which is listed, for details. Allen Carr's Easyway guarantee that you will find it easy to stop smoking at the clinics or your money back.

Allen Carr's Easyway—Worldwide Head Office

Park House, 14 Pepys Road, Raynes Park, London SW20 8NH
Tel: +44 (0)208 944 7761 E-mail: mail@allencarr.com
Website: www.allencarr.com Worldwide Press Office Tel: +44 (0)7970 88 44 52
E-mail: jd@allencarr.com
UK Clinic Information and Central Booking Line 0800 389 2115 (Freephone)

UK Clinics

LONDON
Park House, 14 Pepys Road, Raynes Park, London SW20 8NH
Tel: +44 (0)20 8944 7761
Fax: +44 (0)20 8944 8619
Therapists: John Dicey, Colleen Dwyer, Crispin Hay, Emma Hudson, Rob Fielding, James Pyper
E-mail: mail@allencarr.com
Website: www.allencarr.com

AYLESBURY
Tel: 0800 0197 017
Therapists: Kim Bennett, Emma Hudson
E-mail: kim@easywaybucks.co.uk
Website: www.allencarr.com

BELFAST
Tel: 0845 094 3244
Therapist: Tara Evers-Cheung
E-mail: tara@easywayni.com
Website: www.allencarr.com

BIRMINGHAM
Tel and Fax: +44 (0)121 423 1227
Therapists: John Dicey, Colleen Dwyer, Crispin Hay, Rob Fielding
E-mail: easywayadmin@btconnect.com
Website: www.allencarr.com

BOURNEMOUTH
Tel: 0800 028 7257
Therapist: John Dicey, Colleen Dwyer, Emma Hudson, James Pyper
E-mail: easywayadmin@btconnect.com
Website: www.allencarr.com

BRIGHTON
Tel: 0800 028 7257
Therapists: John Dicey, Colleen Dwyer, Emma Hudson, James Pyper
E-mail: easywayadmin@btconnect.com
Website: www.allencarr.com

BRISTOL
Tel: +44 (0)117 950 1441
Therapist: Charles Holdsworth Hunt
E-mail: stopsmoking@easywaybristol.co.uk
Website: www.allencarr.com

CAMBRIDGE
Tel: 0800 0197 017
Therapists: Kim Bennett, Emma Hudson
E-mail: kim@easywaybucks.co.uk
Website: www.allencarr.com

CARDIFF
Tel: +44 (0)117 950 1441
Therapist: Charles Holdsworth Hunt
E-mail: stopsmoking@easywaybristol.co.uk
Website: www.allencarr.com

COVENTRY
Tel: 0800 321 3007
Therapist: Rob Fielding
E-mail: info@easywaycoventry.co.uk
Website: www.allencarr.com

CREWE
Tel: +44 (0)1270 501 487
Therapist: Debbie Brewer-West
F-mail: debbie@easyway2stopsmoking.co.uk
Website: www.allencarr.com

CUMBRIA
Tel: 0800 077 6187
Therapist: Mark Keen
E-mail: mark@easywaycumbria.co.uk
Website: www.allencarr.com

DERBY
Tel: 01270 50187
Therapists: Debbie Brewer-West
E-mail: debbie@easyway2stopsmoking.co.uk
Website: www.allencarr.com

EXETER
Tel: +44 (0)117 950 1441
Therapist: Charles Holdsworth Hunt
E-mail: stopsmoking@easywayexeter.co.uk
Website: www.allencarr.com

GUERNSEY
Tel: 0800 077 6187
Therapist: Mark Keen
E-mail: mark@easywaylancashire.co.uk
Website: www.allencarr.com

HIGH WYCOMBE
Tel: 0800 0197 017
Therapists: Kim Bennett, Emma Hudson
E-mail: kim@easywaybucks.co.uk
Website: www.allencarr.com

ISLE OF MAN
Tel: 0800 077 6187
Therapist: Mark Keen
E-mail: mark@easywaylancashire.co.uk
Website: www.allencarr.com

JERSEY
Tel: 0800 077 6187
Therapist: Mark Keen
E-mail: mark@easywaylancashire.
co.uk
Website: www.allencarr.com

KENT
Tel: 0800 028 7257
Therapists: John Dicey, Colleen
Dwyer, Emma Hudson, James
Pyper
E-mail: easywayadmin@btconnect.
com
Website: www.allencarr.com

LANCASHIRE
Tel: 0800 077 6187
Therapist: Mark Keen
E-mail: mark@easywaylancashire.
co.uk
Website: www.allencarr.com

LEEDS
Freephone: 0800 804 6796
Therapists: Rob Groves
E-mail: info@easywayyorkshire.
co.uk
Website: www.allencarr.com

LEICESTER
Tel: 0800 321 3007
Therapist: Rob Fielding
E-mail: info@easywayleicester.
co.uk
Website: www.allencarr.com

LIVERPOOL
Tel: 0800 077 6187
Therapist: Mark Keen
E-mail: mark@easywayliverpool.
co.uk
Website: www.allencarr.com

MANCHESTER
Freephone: 0800 804 6796
Therapists: Rob Groves
E-mail: info@easywaymanchester.
co.uk
Website: www.allencarr.com

MILTON KEYNES
Tel: 0800 0197 017
Therapists: Kim Bennett, Emma
Hudson
E-mail: kim@easywaybucks.co.uk
Website: www.allencarr.com

NEWCASTLE/NORTH EAST
Tel/Fax: 0800 077 6187
Therapist: Mark Keen
E-mail: info@easywaynortheast.
co.uk
Website: www.allencarr.com

NORTHAMPTON
Tel: 0800 0197 017
Therapists: Kim Bennett, Emma
Hudson

E-mail: kim@easywaybucks.co.uk
Website: www.allencarr.com

NOTTINGHAM
Tel: 01270 501487
Therapists: Debbie Brewer-West
E-mail: Debbie@
easyway2stopsmoking.co.uk
Website: www.allencarr.com

OXFORD
Tel: 0800 0197 017
Therapists: Kim Bennett, Emma
Hudson
E-mail: kim@easywaybucks.co.uk
Website: www.allencarr.com

PETERBOROUGH
Tel: 0800 0197 017
Therapists: Kim Bennett, Emma
Hudson
E-mail: kim@easywaybucks.co.uk
Website: www.allencarr.com

READING
Tel: 0800 028 7257
Therapist: John Dicey, Colleen Dw-
yer, Emma Hudson, James Pyper
E-mail: easywayadmin@btconnect.
com
Website: www.allencarr.com

SHEFFIELD
Freephone: 0800 804 6796
Therapist: Rob Groves
E-mail:
stopsmoking@easywayyorkshire.
co.uk
Website: www.allencarr.com

SHREWSBURY
Tel: +44 (0)1270 501 487
Therapist: Debbie Brewer-West
E-mail: debbie@easyway-
2stopsmoking.co.uk
Website: www.allencarr.com

SOUTHAMPTON
Tel: 0800 028 7257
Therapists: John Dicey, Colleen
Dwyer, Emma Hudson, James Pyper
E-mail: easywayadmin@btconnect.
com
Website: www.allencarr.com

SOUTHPORT
Tel: 0800 077 6187
Therapist: Mark Keen
E-mail: mark@easywaylancashire.
co.uk
Website: www.allencarr.com

STAINES/HEATHROW
Tel: 0800 028 7257
Therapists: John Dicey, Colleen Dw-
yer, Emma Hudson, James Pyper
E-mail: easywayadmin@btconnect.
com
Website: www.allencarr.com

STEVENAGE
Tel: 0800 019 7017
Therapists: Kim Bennett, Emma
Hudson
E-mail: kim@easywaybucks.co.uk
Website: www.allencarr.com

STOKE
Tel: +44 (0)1270 501 487
Therapist: Debbie Brewer-West
E-mail: debbie@
easyway2stopsmoking.co.uk
Website: www.allencarr.com

SURREY
Park House, 14 Pepys Road, Raynes
Park, London SW20 8NH
Tel : +44 (0)20 8944 7761 Fax:
+44 (0)20 8944 8619
Therapists: John Dicey, Colleen
Dwyer, Crispin Hay, Emma Hud-
son, Rob Fielding, James Pyper
E-mail: mail@allencarr.com
Website: www.allencarr.com

SWINDON
Tel: +44 (0)117 950 1441
Therapist: Charles Holdsworth
Hunt
E-mail: stopsmoking@
easywaybristol.co.uk
Website: www.allencarr.com

TELFORD
Tel: +44 (0)1270 501487
Therapist: Debbie Brewer-West
E-mail: debbie@easyway-
2stopsmoking.co.uk
Website: www.allencarr.com

SCOTLAND
GLASGOW AND EDINBURGH
Tel: +44 (0)131 449 7858
Therapists: Paul Melvin and Jim
McCreadie
E-mail: info@easywayscotland.
co.uk
Website: www.allencarr.com

REPUBLIC OF IRELAND
DUBLIN AND CORK
Lo-Call (From ROI) 1 890 ESYWAY
(37 99 29)
Tel: +353 (0)1 499 9010 (4 lines)
Therapist: Brenda Sweeney and
Team
E-mail: info@allencarr.ie
Website: www.allencarr.com

AUSTRALIA
NORTH QUEENSLAND
Tel: 1300 85 11 75
Therapist: Tara Pickard-Clark
E-mail: nqld@allencarr.com.au
Website: www.allencarr.com

E-mail: kim@easywaybucks.co.uk
Website: www.allencarr.com

SYDNEY, NEW SOUTH WALES
Tel and Fax: 1300 78 51 80
Therapist: Natalie Clays
E-mail: nsw@allencarr.com.au
Website: www.allencarr.com

SOUTH AUSTRALIA
Therapist: Dianne Fisher
Freecall: 1300 55 78 01
E-mail: wa@allencarr.com.au
Website: www.allencarr.com

SOUTH QUEENSLAND
Tel: 1300 85 58 06
Therapist: Jonathan Wills
E-mail: sqld@allencarr.com.au
Website: www.allencarr.com

VICTORIA, TASMANIA, ACT.
Tel: +61 (0)3 9894 8866 or 1300
790 565 (Freecall)
Therapist: Gail Morris
E-mail: info@allencarr.com.au
Website: www.allencarr.com

WESTERN AUSTRALIA
Therapist: Dianne Fisher
Tel: 1300 55 78 01
E-mail: wa@allencarr.com.au
Website: www.allencarr.com

AUSTRIA
SESSIONS HELD THROUGHOUT
AUSTRIA
Free line telephone for Information
and Booking: 0800RAUCHEN
(0800 7282436)
Tel: +43 (0)3512 44755
Therapist: Erich Kellermann and
team
E-mail: info@allen-carr.at
Website: www.allencarr.com

BELGIUM
ANTWERP
Tel: +32 (0)3 281 6255 Fax: +32
(0)3 744 0608.
Therapist: Dirk Nielandt
E-mail: easyway@dirknielandt.be
Website: www.allencarr.com

BULGARIA
Tel: 0800 14104 / +359 899 88 99 07
Therapist: Rumyana Kostadinova
E-mail: rk@nepushaveche.com
Website: www.allencarr.com

CANADA
Toll free 1-866 666 4299 / +1 905
8497736
Therapist: Damian O'Hara
Seminars held in Toronto and
Vancouver
Corporate programs available
throughout Canada
E-mail: info@

theeasywaytostopsmoking.com
Website: www.allencarr.com

CHILE
Tel: +56 2 4744587
Therapist: Claudia Sarmiento
E-mail: contacto@allencarr.cl
Website: www.allencarr.com

COLOMBIA
BOGOTA
Tel: +57 1 245 6910
Therapists: Jose Manuel Duran
E-mail: easywaycolombia@cable.
net.co
Website: www.allencarr.com

CYPRUS
Tel: +357 77 77 78 30
Therapist: Kyriacos Michaelides
E-mail: info@allencarr.com.cy
Website: www.allencarr.com

DENMARK
SESSIONS HELD THROUGHOUT
DENMARK
Tel: +45 70267711
Therapist: Mette Fonss
E-mail: mette@easyway.dk
Website: www.allencarr.com

ECUADOR
Tel and Fax: +593 (0)2 2820 920
Therapist: Ingrid Wittich
E-mail: toisan@pi.pro.ec
Website: www.allencarr.com

ESTONIA
Tel: +372 733 0044
Therapists: Henry Jakobson, Mait
Lõhmus
E-mail: info@allencarr.ee
Website: www.allencarr.com

FRANCE
SESSONS HELD THROUGHOUT
FRANCE
Central Booking Line: **0800
FUMEUR** (Freephone)
Therapists: Erick Serre and Team
Tel: +33 4 91 33 54 55
E-mail: info@allencarr.fr
Website: www.allencarr.com

GERMANY
SESSIONS HELD THROUGHOUT
GERMANY_
Free line telephone for information
and central booking line:
08000RAUCHEN (0800
07282436)
Therapists: Erich Kellermann and
team
Tel: +49 (0)8031 90190-0

E-mail: info@allen-carr.de
Website: www.allencarr.com

GREECE
SESSIONS HELD THROUGHOUT
GREECE
Tel: +30 210 5224087
Therapist: Panos Tzouras
E-mail: panos@allencarr.gr
Website: www.allencarr.com

HONG KONG
Therapist: Rob Groves
Tel: +852 2911 7988
E-mail: stopsmoking@eventclicks.
com
Website: www.allencarr.com

HUNGARY
Website: www.allencarr.com

ICELAND
REYKJAVIK
Tel: +354 553 9590
Therapist: Petur Einarsson
E-mail: easyway@easyway.is
Website: www.allencarr.com

INDIA
BANGALORE AND CHENNAI
Tel: +91 (0)80 41603838
Therapist: Suresh Shottam
E-mail: info@
easywaytostopsmoking.co.in
Website: www.allencarr.com

ISRAEL
SESSIONS HELD THROUGHOUT
ISRAEL
Tel: +972 (0)3 6212525
Therapist/Trainer: Ramy Ro-
manovsky, Orit Rozen, Shahaf Ash-
kenazi, Kinneret Triffon
E-mail: info@allencarr.co.il
Website: www.allencarr.com

ITALY
SESSIONS HELD THROUGHOUT
ITALY
Tel/Fax: +39 (0)2 7060 2438
Therapist: Francesca Cesati and
team
E-mail: info@easywayitalia.com
Website: www.allencarr.com

JAPAN
SESSIONS HELD THROUGHOUT
JAPAN
Visit www.allencarr.com for details.

LATVIA
Tel: +371 67 27 22 25
Therapists: Anatolijs Ivanovs, Eriks Migacevs
E-mail: info@allencarrr.lv
Website: www.allencarr.com

LITHUANIA
Tel: +370 694 29591
Therapist: Evaldas Zvirblis
E-mail: info@mestirukyti.eu
Website: www.allencarr.com

MAURITIUS
Tel: +230 727 5103
Therapist: Heidi Hoareau
E-mail: info@allencarr.mu
Website: www.allencarr.com

MEXICO
SESSIONS HELD THROUGHOUT MEXICO
Tel: +52 55 2623 0631
Therapist: Jorge Davo and Mario Campuzano Otero
E-mail: info@allencarr-mexico.com
Website: www.allencarr.com

NETHERLANDS
SESSIONS HELD THROUGHOUT THE NETHERLANDS
Allen Carr's Easyway "stoppen met roken"
A.C.E. Nederland BV
Buurserstraat 214-216, 7544 RG
ENSCHEDE
The Netherlands
(+31)53 478 43 62
(+31)900 786 77 37
E-mail: info@allencarr.nl
Website: www.allencarr.com

NEW ZEALAND
NORTH ISLAND—AUCKLAND
Tel: +64 (0)9 817 5396
Therapist: Vickie Macrae
E-mail: vickie@easywaynz.co.nz
Website: www.allencarr.com
SOUTH ISLAND—CHRIST-CHURCH
Tel: +64 (0)3 326 5464
Therapist: Laurence Cooke
E-mail: laurence@easywaysouthisland.co.nz
Website: www.allencarr.com

NORWAY
OSLO
Tel: +47 93 20 09 11
Therapist: Rene' Adde
E-mail: post@easyway-norge.no
Website: www.allencarr.com

POLAND
SESSIONS HELD THROUGHOUT POLAND
Tel: +48 (0)22 621 36 11
Therapist: Anna Kabat
E-mail: info@allen-carr.pl
Website: www.allencarr.com

PORTUGAL
OPORTO
Tel: +351 22 9958698
Therapist: Ria Slof
E-mail: info@comodeixardefumar.com
Website: www.allencarr.com

RUSSIA
MOSCOW
Tel: +7 495 644 64 26
Therapist: Fomin Alexander
(Фомин Александр)
ST. PETERSBURG—OPENING 2010/11
E-mail: info@allencarrmoscow.ru
Website: www.allencarr.com

SERBIA
BELGRADE
Tel: +381 (0)11 308 8686
E-mail: office@allencarr.co.rs
E-mail: milos.rakovic@allencarr.co.rs
Website: www.allencarr.com

SINGAPORE
Tel: +65 6329 9660
Therapist: Pam Oei
E-mail: pam@allencarr.com.sg
Website: www.allencarr.com

SLOVENIA
Website: www.allencarr.com

SOUTH AFRICA
SESSIONS HELD THROUGHOUT SOUTH AFRICA
National Booking Line (in SA):
0861 100 200
Head Office: 15 Draper Square, Draper St, Claremont 7708
CAPE TOWN
E-mail: easyway@allencarr.co.za
Website: www.allencarr.com
Therapist: Dr. Charles Nel, Dudley Garner, Malcolm Robinson and Team

SPAIN
MARBELLA
Therapist: Charles Holdsworth Hunt
Tel: +44 8456 187306

E-mail: stopsmoking@easywaymarbella.com
Sessions held in English language
Website: www.allencarr.com

SWEDEN
GOTEBORGE AND MALMÖ
Tel: +46 (0) 8 743 09 50
E-mail: info@allencarr.nu
Website: www.allencarr.com
STOCKHOLM
Tel: +46 (0) 8 743 09 50
Therapist: Christofer Elde
E-mail: info@allencarr.se
Website: www.allencarr.com

SWITZERLAND
SESSIONS HELD THROUGHOUT SWITZERLAND
Free line telephone for information and booking:
0800RAUCHEN (0800 / 728 2436)
Tel: +41 (0)52 383 3773 Fax: +41 (0)52 3833774
Therapist: Cyrill Argast and team
SESSIONS Suisse Romand and Svizzera Italia
Tel: 0800 386 387
E-mail: info@allen-carr.ch
Website: www.allencarr.com

TURKEY
SESSIONS HELD THROUGHOUT TURKEY
Tel: +90 212 358 5307
Trainer: Emre Ustunucar
E-mail: info@allencarrturkiye.com
Website: www.allencarr.com

UKRAINE—OPENING 2010/11
Website: www.allencarr.com

USA
Central information and bookings:
1 866 666 4299
New York: 212-330 9194
E-mail: info@theeasywaytostopsmoking.com
Website: www.allencarr.com
Seminars held regularly in New York, Los Angeles, Denver, and Houston.
Corporate programs available throughout the USA
Mailing address: 1133 Broadway, Suite 706, New York. NY 10010
Therapists: Damian O'Hara, Collene Curran